TACO NIGHT

60+ RECIPES FOR
DATE NIGHTS,
LAZY NIGHTS AND
PARTY NIGHTS

Deborah Kaloper

Smith Street Books

CHICKEN, DUCK & TURKEY

PORK

BEEF & LAMB

INTRODUCTION

▼▼▼

For thousands of years, prehistoric communities in Mexico transformed prized kernels of dried maize into a flat bread they called tlaxcalli. These flat breads were sometimes stuffed with ingredients, depending on what was available – and so the humble taco was born.

Why and when the word taco came into being, remains uncertain. We do know that some millennia later, in the early 16th century, the notorious Spanish conquistador Hernán Cortés would arrange a taco feast in Mexico City for the captains under his command; they greatly admired this finger-licking finger food, as did the waves of Spanish colonists who followed. Around this time tlaxcalli was rechristened tortilla – by Cortés himself, according to some accounts – and a flour-based version was popularised when wheat was introduced from Spain. Despite these centuries of tumult, the spirit and soul of Mexico lives on in the taco's flavourful legacy.

Any US state that shares a border with Mexico has an indelible link to that country's cuisine, giving rise to different permutations such as the Californian burrito and the jalapeno-heavy food known as Tex-Mex. But these days, large chain franchises sling uniform tacos to masses of college students throughout the US. Then there's the rise of upscale Mexican-fusion restaurants, serving trendy tacos and artisanal margaritas at staggering prices. Luckily street-food trucks across the country, and the world over, persist in serving up the classics that speak more truly to the taco's humble origins.

Versatility is the taco's biggest asset. They're breakfast, lunch or dinner (or perhaps all three). They can be eaten one handed, leaving the other hand free for a cold beer. Wherever you're ordering a taco, there's a guarantee of spiciness, crunchiness and glorious greasiness. It's the comfort food for everyone.

But the first thing you need to know is that all tacos start with a tortilla – a round flat bread, which can be made from either corn or flour. The two differ in taste and texture – flour tortillas have a more neutral flavour and are more pliable than their chewy corn cousins.

On the following pages you'll find a breakdown of the myriad chillies mentioned in this book. Then there are instructions on making homemade tortillas, as well as classic taco accoutrements – like refried beans, Mexican green quinoa, various salsas, guacamole and pico de gallo.

The chapters are then separated by your choice of base filling: vegetarian and vegan; seafood; chicken, duck and turkey; pork; and beef and lamb. Simple, right? Within these chapters you'll find traditional fare – such as baja fish (typical of the Tijuana coastline), and the beloved carnitas – as well as modern hybrids, featuring the flavours of a Louisiana Oyster Po' Boy, for example, or the crunch of Vietnamese pork belly banh mi.

Whether you're going for classic or swanky, the simplicity of any taco makes it a great all-rounder: a tasty snack, an ample meal, or the main event at your next informal dinner party.

Most importantly: freestyle it. When dressing each taco, follow your instinct and tastebuds, and don't worry too much about the ratios suggested. If you feel like an entire fistful of guacamole on your shredded brisket – do it. That's what tacos are all about. It's a choose-your-own-adventure story, where all roads lead to yum.

TACO ESSENTIALS

▼▼

You can purchase flour and corn tortillas at most supermarkets, but it's also fun to make your own. With just a few inexpensive ingredients, you can whip up your own dough and roll it into your tortillas of choice, using either a rolling pin or a traditional tortilla press. Then simply heat the tortillas in a cast-iron frying pan or a Mexican comal and serve with your favourite taco fillings.

MASA HARINA

Masa harina (also known as 'masa de harina' or 'maseca') is a specialty corn flour available from Latin-American grocery stores and online. It is made with dried corn that has been soaked and cooked in an alkaline solution, and is required to make tortillas. Regular corn flour or cornmeal will not produce the same results.

FLOUR

Flour tortillas are, unsurprisingly, made with plain (all-purpose) flour. Baking powder helps to slightly leaven the dough and, traditionally, lard is added to make the tortillas soft and pliable, although butter or oil is a perfectly acceptable vegetarian replacement.

COMAL

A comal is a smooth cast-iron flat griddle pan with a shallow edge. It's used throughout Latin America to toast chillies and spices and to cook tortillas – the shallow edge making it easier to flip the tortillas. A regular cast-iron frying pan or heavy-based frying pan is a good alternative.

TORTILLA WARMER

Ranging from round plastic or ceramic containers to insulated cloth pouches, a tortilla warmer will ensure that your tortillas remain warm, soft and pliable for the duration of your taco party. Tortilla warmers come in different sizes and are generally inexpensive. If you don't have one, simply wrap your tortillas in a clean damp tea towel.

TACO PRESS

A taco press makes quick work of preparing tortillas and can also be used to press dough for quesadillas, sopes and more, making it an indispensable utensil in every Mexican kitchen. They can be purchased online and at most Latin American grocery stores.

KEY INGREDIENTS

▼▼▼

CHILLIES

Sweet, fruity, mild or blow-your-head-off spicy, chillies are a fundamental part of Latin American cuisine. Although they are cultivated throughout the world, chillies are native to Mexico and 64 species are grown there today. Used fresh or dried, chillies add depth, complexity and warmth to dishes and sauces.

ANCHO

This large chilli pepper is the dried form of the poblano. The ancho's heat is very mild, allowing its plum, raisin and tobacco flavours to shine. They are heart-shaped and reddish brown to black in colour.

ARBOL

These chillies are long, red, thin and shiny, with an intense heat similar to cayenne. The arbol chilli, also known as chile de àrbol, delivers an earthy burn. They are used in Mexican and Asian cuisine, and globally as a decorative garnish.

BIRD'S EYE

Commonly used in the Keralan region of southern India, and Thailand, these chillies have a tropical burst undercutting their powerful heat. They are named after a dubious likeness to a literal bird's eye, although they're sometimes known as Thai chillies.

CASCABEL

Small and cherry-shaped, the cascabel chilli is deep red when fresh and a dark brown when dried. In Spanish the name translates to 'little bell' or 'sleigh bell', a nod to its shape and the sound its loose seeds make when the dried chilli is shaken. It has a gentle spiciness, and when dried has an earthy, nutty and slightly smoky flavour.

CAYENNE

You can distinguish this pepper by its rippled skin and impressive length. The home cook may have only seen cayenne in its powdered form, but such powders are usually made with the hotter bird's eye chilli or a blend. Try and find the whole cayenne chilli to make use of its natural smokiness.

GUAJILLO

These are dried mirasol chillies. Shiny, and burgundy to brick red in colour, they have a sweet, moderate heat. They taste of fruit and berries with a note of smoky pine. In Central America, guajillo are typically used to flavour chicken-based dishes.

HABANERO

Originally from the depths of the Amazon, the habanero has spread far and wide. Its skin is thin and waxen. It's hot – very, very hot. As such, habaneros are adored by hot sauce fanatics. Habaneros are often confused with their Caribbean cousins, the Scotch bonnet, but do not share their sweetness.

JALAPENO

This chilli pepper is the most widely cultivated in Mexico, making up 30% of the country's chilli production. Typically picked before becoming ripe, jalapeno should remain green and have a moderate heat. They are commonly used in Tex-Mex and, considering their tolerable heat, make an ideal garnish. Chipotle are simply smoke-dried jalapenos.

MORITA

These dried jalapenos are smoked for a relatively short period of time to maintain a soft and silky texture. With a medium heat, morita have flavour notes of sweet red pepper, smoky chocolate, cherry and coffee.

PASILLA

Translating to 'little raisin', that's exactly how the pasilla chilli looks. It's the dried form of the chilaca chilli, with a mild heat and dark, wrinkled skin. The pasilla's herby aroma is contrasted by its licoricey flavour, making it perfect for use in mole sauces.

PEQUIN

These tiny chillies pack a huge punch, although a slightly smoky flavour should be detectable through their heat. Pequins are mostly used for pickling, salsas, soups and vinegars.

POBLANO

These large chillies can be eaten fresh. The poblano's flesh is mild with a slightly grassy flavour. The entire pepper can be stuffed fresh and roasted. When dried, poblano chillies are known as ancho chillies.

DAIRY

Like many countries, the people of Mexico have been making cheese for thousands of years. Fresh, creamy, aged or crumbly, cheese is added to soups, tacos and quesadillas, or sprinkled over elotes, tlayudas or tostadas for a salty, umami hit. Mexican crema is similar to sour cream and is often drizzled over tacos and enchiladas to add creaminess and a slight acidity.

COTIJA CHEESE

This firm white cow's milk cheese from Central Mexico has a dry, crumbly texture and a salty, tangy flavour. When young, cotija has a similar flavour profile to feta. As it ages, the cheese matures in flavour and is often compared to parmesan making it perfect to grate over dishes where a salty, umami taste is required.

MEXICAN CREMA

An indispensable ingredient in Mexican kitchens, Mexican crema is runnier and slightly more acidic than sour cream. To make your own crema, simply warm 250 ml (1 cup) of double (heavy) cream in a saucepan over low heat for a few minutes, then stir through 1 tablespoon of buttermilk. Transfer to a glass jar and let the mixture sit overnight at room temperature until thickened slightly. The next day, add the juice of ½ lime and salt to taste, and store in the fridge for up to a week.

OAXACA CHEESE

Produced in the state of Oaxaca in the southwest of Mexico, oaxaca cheese is a stretched curd cheese with a similar texture and flavour profile to mozzarella. It is a fantastic melting cheese and is often added to quesadillas and stuffed vegetables, such as the cheesy deep-fried zucchini blossoms on page 62.

QUESO FRESCO

Literally meaning 'fresh cheese', queso fresco is a mild, crumbly, milky and slightly acidic cheese found in kitchens throughout Mexico. It is very easy to make at home and is used to top salads, soups, beans and tacos. Because the cheese isn't aged, it only has a short shelf life and should be consumed within 2–3 days. Strained ricotta is a good alternative.

HERBS

Fresh and dried herbs are used throughout Mexican cuisine, but they are not always interchangeable. Coriander is nearly always added as a garnish in its fresh form, while Mexican oregano is generally used dried.

MEXICAN OREGANO

With a flavour profile quite distinct from regular oregano, Mexican oregano is related to lemon verbena, and has grassy, lime citrus notes. It can be bought online and from specialty Latin-American grocery stores. If you are unable to source it, dried marjoram can be used at a pinch.

EPAZOTE

Also known as Mexican tea, epazote is an aromatic herb with a medicinal flavour. Used throughout Mexico in both its fresh and dried form, it is enjoyed for its complex taste and health properties. When cooked with beans, it aids digestion. Dried epazote can be purchased online and at Latin American grocery stores.

FLOUR TORTILLAS

 BASICS

600 g (4 cups) plain (all-purpose) flour

2 teaspoons fine sea salt

1¾ teaspoons baking powder

125 g (4½ oz) lard or butter, finely diced

330 ml (11 fl oz) warm water

Sift the flour, salt and baking powder together into a large bowl.

Add the diced lard or butter and crumble it through the flour until the mixture becomes sand like. Slowly add the water, little by little, while kneading the mixture together until it forms an elastic dough.

Divide the dough into 18 equal portions, roll into balls, then cover with a clean tea towel and leave to rest for 30–40 minutes.

Place a ball of dough between two pieces of waxed baking paper and use a rolling pin to roll it out into an 18 cm (7 inch) round tortilla. Continue rolling out all of the tortillas, then cover with the tea towel until ready to cook.

Heat a large flat cast-iron frying pan or comal over medium–high heat. Add a tortilla and cook for 1–1½ minutes on each side, until the tortilla is slightly dry to the touch, with lightly browned bubbles on the surface; it should feel dry, but still be soft and pliable.

While cooking the remaining tortillas, keep the cooked tortillas warm by stacking them on top of each other and covering them with the tea towel.

Serve immediately.

NOTE

For a fresh twist, try making chilli flake or marigold petal tortillas. While rolling out the tortillas, sprinkle the top of the dough with a pinch of chilli flakes, or edible marigold petals.

CORN TORTILLAS

 BASICS

220 g (2 cups) masa harina
375 ml (1½ cups) warm water
2 teaspoons fine sea salt

Place the ingredients in a large bowl and, using your hands, mix together until a dough forms. It should be pliable, almost like a play dough; add a little more water if it's a bit dry.

Knead the dough for 1–2 minutes, then divide into 16 equal portions. Roll into balls, then cover with a clean tea towel and leave to rest for 20–30 minutes.

Place a ball of dough between two pieces of waxed baking paper and use a rolling pin to roll it out into a 15 cm (6 inch) round tortilla. (If you have a tortilla press, place a piece of waxed baking paper on the base plate, then place the dough ball in the centre and add another piece of waxed baking paper on top. Close the tortilla press and press the handle down to sandwich and flatten the dough into a tortilla.)

Continue rolling or pressing until all the balls have been flattened to size. Cover with the tea towel until ready to cook.

Heat a large flat cast-iron frying pan or comal over medium–high heat. Add a tortilla and flip after 10 seconds, then cook for 45–60 seconds. Flip again and cook for a further 35–50 seconds. The tortilla should feel dry, but not stiff or crumbly, and should be just lightly changed in colour.

While cooking the remaining tortillas, keep the cooked tortillas warm by stacking them on top of each other and covering them with the tea towel.

Serve immediately.

NOTE

To make beetroot or spinach corn tortillas, replace 60 ml (¼ cup) of the water with fresh beetroot (beet) juice or spinach juice, for a colourful twist.

FLOUR TORTILLAS

CORN TORTILLAS

BEANS IN THE POT

BASICS

250 g (9 oz) dried pinto or black beans, soaked overnight in plenty of cold water

1 onion, diced

1 bay leaf

2–3 garlic cloves, peeled and smashed

1½ teaspoons dried epazote (see Note)

1 tablespoon sea salt

Drain the soaked beans and place in a large saucepan with the onion, bay leaf and garlic cloves. Cover with 7.5–10 cm (3–4 inches) of water and bring to the boil over high heat.

Reduce the heat and simmer, stirring occasionally, for 45 minutes to 1 hour, until the beans are tender.

Stir in the epazote and salt and cook for a further 10–15 minutes, until the beans are completely cooked through. Serve immediately.

NOTE

Epazote is a herb used in Mexican cuisine. It can be purchased from specialty grocery stores and online.

REFRIED BEANS

BASICS

80 ml (⅓ cup) vegetable oil or lard

1 small onion, peeled and halved

50 g (1¾ oz) piece of salted smoked pork (optional)

600 g (3½ cups) cooked pinto or black beans (see Note)

170 ml (⅔ cup) cooking liquid reserved from the beans, or chicken stock or water

TO SERVE

crumbled cheese, such as cotija, oaxaca, queso fresco, feta, mozzarella or ricotta

Warm the oil or lard in a large heavy-based saucepan over medium heat. Add the onion and smoked pork, if using. Heat through to flavour the oil for 1–2 minutes, then remove the onion and smoked pork and reserve for another use.

Add the beans and stir the flavoured oil through, then cook for 5–8 minutes.

Smash the beans with a potato masher, or the back of a large spoon. Add the reserved bean cooking liquid or stock or water as needed, to achieve the desired consistency and creaminess, cooking for a further 4–5 minutes to warm the beans through.

Season to taste with sea salt and serve immediately, with a sprinkling of your favourite cheese.

NOTE

If cooking the beans from scratch, start with 250 g (9 oz) dried beans; soak them overnight and cook as directed for the Beans in the pot recipe opposite.

CHARRO BEANS (AKA COWBOY BEANS)

 BASICS

2 teaspoons olive oil

180 g (6½ oz) Mexican chorizo sausages, removed from their casings

180 g (6½ oz) kaiserfleisch or smoked ham, cut into 1 cm (½ inch) dice

½ large onion, cut into 1 cm (½ inch) dice

2 fresh green jalapeno chillies, finely diced

2–3 large garlic cloves, crushed

1 tablespoon ground cumin

2 teaspoons dried epazote (see Note)

400 g (14 oz) tin chopped fire-roasted tomatoes

750 ml (3 cups) beef or chicken stock

1 bay leaf

1 kg (6 cups) cooked or tinned pinto beans

warm tortillas, to serve

Place a large saucepan over medium heat. Add the olive oil and saute the chorizo and ham for 1–2 minutes, breaking up the sausage as it browns, then add the onion and cook for a further 3–4 minutes.

Add the jalapeno chilli, garlic, cumin and epazote, stirring to combine. Stir in the tomatoes, stock and bay leaf and bring to the boil. Reduce the heat to a simmer, add the beans and cook for 15–20 minutes, to allow the flavours to combine.

Season to taste with sea salt and black pepper. Serve with warm tortillas.

NOTE

Epazote is a herb used in Mexican cuisine. It can be purchased from specialty grocery stores or online.

MEXICAN RED RICE

 BASICS

60 ml (¼ cup) olive oil

400 g (2 cups) long-grain white rice

I small onion, diced

I small carrot, diced

I large garlic clove, crushed

125 g (½ cup) tomato passata (pureed tomatoes)

750 ml (3 cups) chicken stock, vegetable stock or water

2 teaspoons fine sea salt

80 g (½ cup) peas (blanched if fresh, thawed if frozen)

Warm the olive oil in a saucepan over medium heat. Add the rice and stir to coat the grains with the oil. Cook, stirring, for 5–6 minutes.

Add the onion and carrot and cook for a further 5–6 minutes, then add the garlic and stir constantly for 1–2 minutes, until the onion is translucent and soft.

Add the passata, stock and salt, stirring to combine.

Bring to the boil, then reduce the heat, cover and simmer for 15 minutes, or until all the liquid has been absorbed and the rice is tender. Stir in the peas to warm through before serving.

CHICHARRONES

MEXICAN GREEN QUINOA

CHARRO BEANS

MEXICAN RED RICE

CHICHARRONES

 BASICS

500 g (1 lb 2 oz) pork skin, or pork crackling, scored and cut into 3 cm (1¼ inch) wide strips

1 tablespoon sea salt flakes

2 teaspoons chilli powder

vegetable oil, for deep-frying

Preheat the oven to 150°C (300°F).

Place the cut strips of pork skin, fat side down, on a wire rack set over a deep baking tray (to catch the melting fat). Transfer to the oven and bake for 1 hour.

Reduce the oven temperature to 120°C (250°F), or as low as it will go, and bake for a further 1½ hours to dry the pork skin out.

In a small bowl, combine the salt flakes and chilli powder. Set aside.

In a large saucepan, heat enough oil for deep-frying to 180°C (350°F). Carefully fry the pork strips a few at a time, taking care as the hot oil may spit. Cook for 45–60 seconds, or until the pork strips puff up and are golden brown in colour.

Remove with a slotted spoon to a wire rack and dust with the chilli salt.

Serve immediately, or store in a clean airtight container at cool room temperature and use within 3–4 days.

MEXICAN GREEN QUINOA

200 g (I cup) white quinoa

45 g (I cup) finely shredded baby spinach leaves

45 g (I cup) finely shredded baby kale leaves

2 spring onions (scallions), thinly sliced

¼ cup finely shredded mint leaves

¼ cup chopped coriander (cilantro) leaves

I fresh green jalapeno chilli, finely diced

30 g (¼ cup) slivered pistachios

30 g (¼ cup) pumpkin seeds (pepitas)

60 ml (¼ cup) extra virgin olive oil

juice and zest of I lemon

Rinse the quinoa and place in a saucepan. Pour in 500 ml (2 cups) of water and bring to the boil over high heat. Stir, then reduce the heat to a simmer, cover and cook for 12 minutes.

Remove the pan from the heat and leave to sit with the lid on for a further 10 minutes.

Fluff the quinoa with a fork, then place in a large serving bowl and allow to cool slightly.

Add the remaining ingredients and season with sea salt and black pepper. Toss to combine, then serve.

ROASTED CORN and BLACK BEAN SALSA

2 corn cobs, husks and silks removed

125 g (¾ cup) cooked black beans

1 fresh green jalapeno chilli, finely diced; leave the seeds in if you like the heat

1 small red bird's eye chilli, seeds removed (optional), thinly sliced

½ red onion, finely diced

125 g (4½ oz) cherry tomatoes, quartered

¼ cup finely chopped coriander (cilantro) leaves

¼ cup finely chopped mint leaves

zest and juice of 1 large lime

1 tablespoon extra virgin olive oil

Place a chargrill pan over medium–high heat. Grill the corn cobs, turning on all sides, for 7–10 minutes, until slightly blackened and just cooked.

Allow the corn to cool slightly, then carefully remove the kernels from the cobs using a sharp knife.

Place all the ingredients in a bowl, toss to combine and season with sea salt and black pepper to taste.

Refrigerate in a clean airtight container until required; the salsa is best served on the day it is made.

TOMATILLO SALSA VERDE

500 g (1 lb 2 oz) tomatillos, husks removed, rinsed

½ onion

3 garlic cloves

3 fresh green jalapeno chillies, stems removed, seeds scooped out

1 teaspoon sea salt

1 cup roughly chopped coriander (cilantro) leaves and stems

For a fresh salsa verde, roughly chop the tomatillos and onion and place in a food processor. Peel the garlic and add to the processor, along with the remaining ingredients, and blend until well pureed.

For a roasted salsa verde, place the tomatillos, unpeeled onion and unpeeled garlic cloves on a baking tray. Cut the chillies in half lengthways and add to the tray, then place the tray under an oven grill (broiler) on high heat. Grill for 9–10 minutes, until the ingredients are slightly charred and beginning to blacken in spots, then turn them over and cook for a further 6–7 minutes, until charred. Remove from the heat and leave to cool slightly. Peel the onion and garlic, then place in a food processor with the chillies. Add the remaining ingredients and blend until pureed. Use straight away, or cool before refrigerating.

The salsa verde can be refrigerated in a clean airtight container for 5–7 days.

FRESH TOMATO SALSA

 SALSAS, PICKLES & SAUCES

400 g (14 oz) ripe tomatoes, roughly chopped

1 fresh red jalapeno chilli

½ small red onion, roughly chopped

2 garlic cloves

1 teaspoon sea salt

1½ tablespoons lime juice

¼ cup chopped coriander (cilantro) leaves

Place all the ingredients in a blender and blitz until coarsely chopped to a chunky consistency.

The salsa will keep in a clean airtight container in the fridge for 2–3 days.

NOTE

This simple salsa is best made when tomatoes are in season, to allow their bright flavour to shine through.

ROASTED TOMATO SALSA

SALSAS, PICKLES & SAUCES

400 g (14 oz) ripe tomatoes

1 fresh red jalapeno chilli

½ small red onion, unpeeled

2 garlic cloves, unpeeled

1 teaspoon sea salt

1½ tablespoons lime juice

¼ cup chopped coriander (cilantro) leaves

Place a cast-iron frying pan or chargrill pan over high heat and add the tomatoes, chilli, onion half and garlic cloves. Roast the garlic, turning occasionally, for 6–7 minutes, and the tomatoes, chilli and onion for 12–14 minutes, until blackened, charred and softly roasted.

Allow to cool, then peel the onion and garlic and add to a blender with the remaining ingredients. Blitz until coarsely chopped, or to your liking. Taste and adjust the seasoning if desired.

The salsa will keep in an airtight container in the fridge for 2–3 days.

NOTE

If you're worried about the heat from the chilli, you can remove the seeds before blending the salsa, then gradually add them in to achieve the desired degree of heat.

MANGO SALSA

1 large mango, peeled and stoned, flesh cut into 1 cm (½ inch) cubes

½ small red onion, diced

½ fresh green jalapeno chilli, finely diced; leave the seeds in if you like the heat

¼ cup chopped coriander (cilantro) leaves

zest and juice of 1 large lime

Place all the ingredients in a bowl and gently toss to combine.

Refrigerate in a clean airtight container until required; the salsa is best served on the day it is made.

AVOCADO TOMATILLO SAUCE (TAQUERIA STYLE)

½ large avocado

½ quantity Tomatillo salsa verde (page 28)

80 ml (⅓ cup) lime juice

1 fresh green jalapeno chilli, roughly chopped; leave the seeds in if you like the heat

Place the ingredients in a blender and puree until smooth. For a thinner sauce, blend in 1–2 tablespoons of water.

Refrigerate the sauce in a clean airtight container for 3–4 days.

NOTE

For a richer, creamier sauce, add 80 g (⅓ cup) of Mexican crema, sour cream or creme fraiche.

PINEAPPLE SALSA

~~~~~~~~◆~~~~~~~~◆ SALSAS, PICKLES & SAUCES ◆~~~~~~~~◆~~~~~~~~

320 g (11½ oz) fresh pineapple, cut into 1 cm (½ inch) dice

¼ red onion, thinly sliced

1 fresh green jalapeno chilli, finely chopped

1 tablespoon chopped coriander (cilantro) leaves

1 tablespoon chopped mint leaves

zest and juice of 1 large lime (approximately)

Combine the ingredients in a bowl. Taste and adjust the amount of lime juice to your liking, then season with sea salt and black pepper to taste.

The salsa will keep in a clean airtight container in the fridge for 2 days.

NOTE

Instead of a jalapeno chilli, you could use 3 dried pequin chillies. Simply dry-roast the chillies in a cast-iron frying pan over medium–high heat until softened, then grind into a powder using a spice grinder; you should end up with about ¼ teaspoon chilli powder.

PICO DE GALLO

~~~~~~~~◆~~~~~~~~◆ SALSAS, PICKLES & SAUCES ◆~~~~~~~~◆~~~~~~~~

3 large ripe juicy tomatoes, diced

½ white onion, diced

1 fresh green jalapeno chilli, finely diced

1 small garlic clove, crushed

½ cup chopped coriander (cilantro) leaves

60 ml (¼ cup) lime juice

Add the ingredients to a bowl and mix until well combined. Season with sea salt and black pepper to taste.

The pico de gallo is best made near serving time, but will keep refrigerated in a clean airtight container for 1 day.

GUACAMOLE

2 large ripe avocados, diced and mashed

¼ red onion, finely diced

2 tablespoons lime juice

½ fresh green jalapeno chilli, finely diced

2 tablespoons finely chopped coriander (cilantro) leaves

Place the ingredients in a bowl, mix to combine and season with sea salt to taste.

Refrigerate in a clean airtight container until required; the guacamole is best served on the day it is made.

PICKLED RED ONION

2 red onions, thinly sliced

2 garlic cloves, thinly sliced

2 red bird's eye chillies, split

2 allspice berries

1 bay leaf

¼ teaspoon black peppercorns

2 teaspoons sea salt

3 tablespoons white granulated sugar

250 ml (1 cup) apple cider vinegar

125 ml (½ cup) lime juice

Place the onion in a heatproof bowl and cover with boiling water. Let sit for 20–30 seconds, then drain and refresh under cold water.

Place the onion in a large clean glass jar with the remaining ingredients, then seal and refrigerate for at least 2 hours before using.

The pickled onion will keep in the fridge for up to 2 weeks.

PINEAPPLE SALSA

PICO DE GALLO

GUACAMOLE

PICKLED RED ONION

PICKLED TAQUERIA-STYLE VEGETABLES

SALSAS, PICKLES & SAUCES

I carrot, sliced into coins

6 fresh green jalapeno chillies, halved, seeds removed

125 g (1 cup) small cauliflower florets

¼ white onion, sliced

6 radishes, quartered

250 ml (1 cup) white vinegar

I bay leaf

½ teaspoon dried Mexican oregano (see Note)

¼ teaspoon black peppercorns

I tablespoon sea salt

I tablespoon white sugar

Combine the ingredients in a saucepan over medium heat. Stir in 250 ml (1 cup) of water and simmer for 10–12 minutes.

Allow to cool, then transfer the mixture to a large clean glass jar, seal and refrigerate.

The pickles will keep in the fridge for up to 2 weeks.

NOTE

Dried Mexican oregano can be purchased online and from Latin American grocery stores.

BLOW-YOUR-HEAD-OFF HABANERO HOT SAUCE

SALSAS, PICKLES & SAUCES

2 garlic cloves

125 ml (½ cup) white vinegar

1 small carrot, grated

1 small onion, diced

80 g (about 10) fresh habanero chillies, stems removed, seeds left in

1 ripe orange heirloom tomato, roughly chopped

1½ teaspoons sea salt

1 teaspoon panela (see Note) or brown sugar

Dry-roast the garlic cloves in a frying pan over low heat for 5–10 minutes, turning occasionally, until the skins are lightly blackened and charred.

Transfer the garlic to a saucepan, along with the rest of the ingredients. Stir in 125 ml (½ cup) of water and simmer over medium heat for 10–15 minutes, until the chillies and onion are soft and cooked through.

Allow to cool, then puree the ingredients in a high-speed blender to a smooth consistency.

The sauce will keep in a clean airtight container in the fridge for 5–7 days.

NOTE

Panela is an unrefined cane sugar, typically used in Latin American recipes.

BLOW-YOUR-HEAD-OFF HABANERO HOT SAUCE

PICKLED TAQUERIA-STYLE VEGETABLES

RED CHILLI SAUCE

GREEN CHILLI SAUCE

RED CHILLI SAUCE

SALSAS, PICKLES & SAUCES

12 dried arbol chillies

2 dried guajillo chillies

2 large garlic cloves, unpeeled

1 large ripe heirloom tomato

2 tablespoons white vinegar

1 teaspoon sea salt

Warm a cast-iron frying pan over low heat and dry-fry the chillies, in batches, for 1 minute on each side, taking care to not burn the skin. Remove and set aside. When cool enough to handle, discard the stems and seeds, or retain some seeds if you prefer a spicier chilli sauce.

Place the chillies in a bowl, then cover with boiling water and leave to rehydrate for 20 minutes. Drain, reserving 2 tablespoons of the chilli soaking water.

Meanwhile, dry-roast the garlic cloves and whole tomato in the pan, turning occasionally, for 5–10 minutes, until the skins are lightly blackened and charred.

Peel the garlic cloves and add to a high-speed blender with the remaining ingredients, including the reserved chilli soaking water. Blitz to a puree.

The sauce will keep in a clean airtight container in the fridge for 5–7 days.

GREEN CHILLI SAUCE

 SALSAS, PICKLES & SAUCES

200 g (7 oz) fresh green jalapeno chillies, roughly chopped

4 fresh green cayenne chillies, roughly chopped

1 white onion, roughly chopped

1 cup roughly chopped coriander (cilantro) leaves

2 large garlic cloves, roughly chopped

125 ml (½ cup) white vinegar

60 ml (¼ cup) lime juice

2 tablespoons panela (see Notes) or brown sugar

2½ teaspoons sea salt

Place the ingredients in a high-speed blender, add 80 ml (⅓ cup) of water and puree until smooth.

The sauce will keep in a clean airtight container in the fridge for 3–4 days.

NOTES

Panela is an unrefined cane sugar, typically used in Latin American recipes.

For a less acidic sauce with a milder flavour, heat 125 ml (½ cup) of vegetable oil in a saucepan over medium heat, then carefully add the raw green chilli sauce – it will spit! Cook for 4–5 minutes, then leave to cool. The sauce will keep in a clean airtight container in the fridge for 5–7 days.

CHIPOTLE ADOBO JACKFRUIT

XXXXXXXXXXXXXXXXXXXXXXX VEGETARIAN & VEGAN XXXXXXXXXXXXXXXXXXXXXXX

2 × 565 g (1 lb 4 oz) tins jackfruit in brine, drained and rinsed (see Note)

1 tablespoon olive oil

1 onion, thinly sliced

4 garlic cloves, crushed

1 teaspoon each ground cumin, smoked paprika, ancho chilli powder and sea salt

½ teaspoon ground cinnamon

4 chipotle chillies in adobo sauce, plus 3 tablespoons of the sauce

400 g (14 oz) tin chopped tomatoes

250 ml (1 cup) vegetable stock

60 ml (¼ cup) white vinegar

1 tablespoon brown sugar

VEGAN CREMA

300 g (10½ oz) silken tofu, drained

3 tablespoons lime juice

1 tablespoon lime zest

1 tablespoon olive oil

1 tablespoon apple cider vinegar

1 teaspoon sea salt

½ teaspoon each chilli powder, garlic powder and onion powder

⅓ cup chopped coriander (cilantro)

TO SERVE

¼ white cabbage, shredded

12 warm Corn tortillas (page 15)

1 avocado, diced

coriander (cilantro) leaves

12 lime wedges

Mexican red rice (page 21)

Beans in the pot (page 18)

To make the crema, place all the ingredients in a blender and process until smooth. Taste and adjust the seasoning to your liking, adding more lime juice or chilli powder as desired. Refrigerate until required; the crema will keep in a clean airtight container in the fridge for 3–4 days, and makes about 375 g (1½ cups).

Place the drained jackfruit in a large bowl. Use your fingers to shred the fruit into strands, then set aside.

Warm the oil in a large frying pan over medium heat. Saute the onion for 4–5 minutes, then stir in the garlic and ground spices and saute for a further 1–1½ minutes.

Add the remaining ingredients, along with the shredded jackfruit, stirring to combine. Reduce the heat to low and simmer slowly for 25–30 minutes, until the flavours are well combined and the sauce has thickened and reduced.

To serve, place some shredded cabbage on a warm tortilla, then top with some jackfruit mixture and avocado. Drizzle with some of the crema and garnish with coriander. Finish with a squeeze of lime and serve immediately, with rice and beans on the side.

NOTE

You'll need about 550 g (1 lb 3 oz) drained jackfruit.

TURMERIC SCRAMBLED TOFU *and* SPINACH

2 tablespoons coconut oil

½ teaspoon ground turmeric

1½ teaspoons ground cumin

250 g (9 oz) firm tofu, well drained (see Note) and crumbled

1 garlic clove, crushed

1 chipotle chilli in adobo sauce, chopped, plus 2 tablespoons of the sauce

90 g (2 cups) chopped baby spinach leaves

TO SERVE

12 warm Beetroot (beet) corn tortillas (page 15)

Roasted corn & black bean salsa (page 28)

Guacamole (page 35)

coriander (cilantro) leaves (optional)

Mexican red rice (page 21)

Warm the coconut oil in a frying pan over medium heat. Add the turmeric, cumin, tofu and garlic and fry together for 1–2 minutes.

Add the chilli, adobo sauce, spinach and 60 ml (¼ cup) of water. Cook, stirring, for another few minutes, until the water has evaporated and the spinach has wilted through.

To serve, spoon some of the scrambled tofu onto a warm tortilla, then top with some salsa, guacamole and coriander, if desired. Serve immediately, with red rice.

NOTE

To drain the tofu, place it on top of several sheets of paper towel, place more sheets of paper towel on top, then weigh it down with a heavy plate and leave to drain. Squeeze out the excess water before using.

VEGAN NUTTY PICADILLO

50 g (½ cup) walnuts

80 g (½ cup) blanched almonds

100 g (½ cup) cooked or tinned lentils

2 tablespoons olive oil

2 teaspoons tamari

2 tablespoons chopped coriander (cilantro) leaves

1 teaspoon ground cumin

½ teaspoon ancho chilli powder

¼ teaspoon onion powder

¼ teaspoon garlic powder

¼ teaspoon fine sea salt

¼ teaspoon cracked black pepper

TO SERVE

shredded iceberg lettuce

12 warm Corn tortillas (page 15)

shredded vegan cheese

Pico de gallo (page 34)

Avocado tomatillo sauce (page 32)

Place the walnuts and almonds in a blender and pulse into crumbs. Add the remaining ingredients and pulse to combine.

To serve, place some shredded lettuce on a warm tortilla, then add some of the picadillo mixture. Top with cheese and pico di gallo, drizzle with avocado tomatillo sauce and serve immediately.

GOCHUJANG TOFU *with* KIMCHI *and* AVOCADO

VEGETARIAN & VEGAN

500 g (1 lb 2 oz) firm tofu, sliced into 8 even pieces

1 tablespoon olive oil

1 tablespoon toasted sesame oil

GOCHUJANG SAUCE

60 g (¼ cup) gochujang paste

3 tablespoons tomato ketchup

2 tablespoons honey

1 tablespoon soy sauce

2–3 garlic cloves, minced

2 teaspoons minced ginger

½ teaspoon chilli flakes

TO SERVE

2 handfuls of finely shredded purple cabbage

8 warm small Flour tortillas (page 14)

kimchi

1 large avocado, sliced

Spicy lime crema (page 85)

coriander (cilantro) leaves

black sesame seeds

lime wedges

Pat the tofu dry with paper towel, pressing out the excess moisture.

Place a large cast-iron frying pan over medium–high heat. Add the olive and sesame oils.

Working in batches, fry the tofu for about 1½ minutes on each side, until golden brown. Transfer to a plate and set aside, keeping the pan handy.

In a bowl, mix together the gochujang sauce ingredients and 2 tablespoons of water, then pour into the same pan you fried the tofu in. Gently warm the sauce over medium–low heat.

Gently toss the fried tofu slices through the sauce, drenching them with sauce.

To serve, place some shredded cabbage on a warm tortilla, then top with a tofu slice, some kimchi and avocado. Drizzle with a little lime crema. Scatter over coriander leaves and black sesame seeds. Serve immediately, with lime wedges.

RAJAS POBLANAS *and* CORN

300 g (10½ oz) fresh poblano chillies

2 tablespoons olive oil

15 g (½ oz) butter

1 onion, thinly sliced

300 g (1½ cups) fresh corn kernels

1 garlic clove, crushed

125 g (½ cup) Mexican crema, sour cream or creme fraiche

125 g (½ cup) queso requeson or ricotta

zest of 1 lemon

TO SERVE

12 warm Spinach corn tortillas (page 15)

cotija, ricotta salata or goat's cheese

2½ tablespoons pumpkin seeds (pepitas), toasted

coriander (cilantro) leaves

12 lemon wedges

Beans in the pot (page 18)

Mexican green quinoa (page 25)

Heat an oven grill (broiler) to medium–high. Place the chillies on a baking tray and grill (broil) for 7–8 minutes on each side, until the skin has blackened and is charred in spots, and the flesh is soft. Place the chillies in a bowl and cover with plastic wrap. When cool enough to handle, remove the stems and seeds from the chillies, and peel off and discard the skins. Cut the chillies into thin strips and set aside.

Warm the olive oil and butter in a large frying pan over medium–high heat. When the butter has melted, saute the onion for 4 minutes, then add the corn and saute for a further 3–4 minutes. Finally, add the garlic and roasted chilli strips and saute for 1–2 minutes.

Reduce the heat slightly, then stir in the crema, cheese and lemon zest until combined. Cook for 1–2 minutes, until warmed through and creamy. Season to taste with sea salt and black pepper.

To serve, spoon some of the corn mixture onto a warm tortilla. Crumble some cheese over, garnish with a scattering of pumpkin seeds and coriander, then finish with a squeeze of lemon. Serve immediately, with beans in the pot and Mexican green quinoa.

HALOUMI *with* POMEGRANATE SALSA *and* CHILLI DUKKAH

1½ tablespoons olive oil

240 g (8½ oz) haloumi, sliced into 16 even pieces

½ lemon, plus lemon wedges to serve

16 warm small blue corn tortillas

handful of rocket (arugula) leaves

2 radishes, thinly sliced

CHILLI DUKKAH

50 g (⅓ cup) raw whole almonds

50 g (⅓ cup) raw shelled pistachios

2–3 tablespoons sesame seeds

1 tablespoon cumin seeds

1 tablespoon coriander seeds

2 teaspoons Aleppo chilli flakes

1½ teaspoons sea salt flakes

1 teaspoon Urfa biber chilli flakes

⅛–¼ teaspoon cayenne pepper

TAHINI YOGHURT

125 g (½ cup) Greek-style yoghurt

3 tablespoons tahini

3 tablespoons lemon juice

small handful of chopped mint leaves

POMEGRANATE SALSA

seeds from ½ large pomegranate

½ red onion, diced

¼ fresh green jalapeno chilli, finely diced

1 tablespoon chopped mint leaves

2 teaspoons lime juice

½ teaspoon extra virgin olive oil

Preheat the oven to 180ºC (350ºF).

To make the chilli dukkah, spread the almonds and pistachios on a baking tray and roast for about 7 minutes, taking care they don't burn. Tip into a bowl and set aside to cool completely.

Add the sesame, cumin and coriander seeds to a cast-iron frying pan and place over medium heat. Toast the seeds for about 3 minutes, until fragrant and lightly golden. Remove from the heat and cool completely.

Using a mortar and pestle, pound the toasted nuts and seeds with the remaining dukkah ingredients until broken down into small pebbles. The dukkah will keep in a sealed glass container in the pantry for 3–4 weeks.

To make the tahini yoghurt, combine the yoghurt, tahini and lemon juice in a bowl and whisk well to combine. Taste and add a little more lemon juice or water to thin the sauce if desired. Stir through the mint, then cover and refrigerate until ready to use; it will keep for 4–5 days.

Combine the pomegranate salsa ingredients in a bowl, mixing well. Cover and refrigerate until ready to serve (the salsa is best consumed on the day it is made).

Place a large cast-iron frying pan over medium heat and add the olive oil. Pat the haloumi pieces dry with paper towel. Fry the haloumi, in batches if needed, for 1–1½ minutes on each side, until the cheese is soft and golden brown. Remove from the heat and squeeze the lemon juice over.

To serve, spoon a little tahini yoghurt onto a warm double-stacked tortilla. Top with rocket, two haloumi pieces, then some pomegranate salsa and radish slices. Sprinkle with dukkah and serve immediately, with lemon wedges.

SAUTEED MUSHROOM *and* ASHED GOAT'S CHEESE

115 g (4 oz) butter

3 tablespoons olive oil

300 g (10½ oz) shiitake mushrooms, or your favourite mushrooms, sliced

5 large garlic cloves, thinly sliced

1½ teaspoons chopped thyme leaves

½ teaspoon chopped oregano leaves

2½ tablespoons pine nuts, toasted

12 silverbeet (Swiss chard) or rainbow chard leaves (about 180 g/6½ oz), shredded

zest and juice of 1 lemon

DUKKAH

50 g (⅓ cup) raw whole almonds, toasted

2 tablespoons coriander seeds

2 tablespoons cumin seeds

2 teaspoons black cumin seeds

80 g (½ cup) sesame seeds

½ teaspoon fine sea salt

½ teaspoon cracked black pepper

TO SERVE

12 warm Corn tortillas (page 15)

125 g (4½ oz) ashed goat's cheese

extra virgin olive oil, for drizzling

lemon zest

lemon wedges

Green chilli sauce (page 43) or Roasted tomatillo salsa verde (page 28)

Preheat the oven to 180°C (350°F).

To make the dukkah, spread the almonds on a baking tray and roast for about 7 minutes, taking care they don't burn. Tip into a bowl and set aside to cool completely.

Add the coriander and both types of cumin seeds to a cast-iron frying pan and place over medium heat. Toast the seeds for about 3 minutes, until fragrant and lightly golden. Remove from the heat and cool completely, then repeat with the sesame seeds.

Place the almonds, coriander seeds and cumin seeds in a spice grinder and roughly blitz, or use a mortar and pestle to pound and roughly crush them together. Place in a bowl with the sesame seeds, salt and pepper, and mix to combine. The dukkah will keep in a clean airtight container at cool room temperature for 3–4 weeks, and makes about 150 g (1¼ cups).

Warm the butter and olive oil in a large frying pan over medium–high heat. When the butter has melted, saute the mushrooms for 1–2 minutes, then add the garlic, thyme and oregano and saute for a further 1–2 minutes. Season with sea salt and black pepper. Add the pine nuts, tossing them through. Transfer the mixture to a large bowl and keep warm.

Add the silverbeet to the same pan, stirring to coat in the remaining pan oil. Add the lemon zest and juice, stirring for a minute or two, until the silverbeet has just wilted. Fold the silverbeet through the mushroom mixture.

To serve, place some of the sauteed mushroom mixture on a warm tortilla. Crumble over some goat's cheese, drizzle with olive oil and sprinkle with a pinch of the dukkah. Finish with a little lemon zest, a squeeze of lemon juice and a splash of green chilli sauce or salsa verde. Serve immediately.

MAPLE CHILLI-ROASTED SWEET POTATO

XXXXXXXXXXXXXXXXXXXXXXXXXX VEGETARIAN & VEGAN XXXXXXXXXXXXXXXXXXXXXXXXXX

2–3 sweet potatoes (about 800 g/1 lb 12 oz), cut into 3 cm (1¼ inch) cubes

2 tablespoons olive oil

2 tablespoons maple syrup

1 teaspoon chilli powder

1 teaspoon chilli flakes

1 teaspoon ground cumin

½ teaspoon garlic powder

½ teaspoon onion powder

½ teaspoon smoked paprika

½ teaspoon salt flakes

AVOCADO CREMA

1 large avocado

1 large garlic clove, peeled

75 ml (2½ fl oz) lime juice

2 tablespoons Mexican crema or sour cream

2–3 teaspoons pickled jalapeno juice from the jar

TO SERVE

rocket (arugula) leaves

8 warm Corn tortillas (page 15)

Roasted corn & black bean salsa (page 28)

100 g (3½ oz) goat's cheese, crumbled

lime wedges

To make the avocado crema, slice the avocado in half, remove the stone and scoop the flesh into a small blender or food processor. Add the remaining ingredients and a good pinch of sea salt and blitz until smooth, adding 2–3 tablespoons of water a little at a time if you'd like a thinner consistency. (Alternatively, use a mortar and pestle to blend the ingredients.) The crema will keep in a sealed glass container in the fridge for 4–5 days.

Preheat the oven to 200°C (400°F). Line a baking tray with baking paper.

In a bowl, toss the sweet potato cubes in the olive oil and season with sea salt and black pepper. Spread them in an even layer on the baking tray, then roast for 20 minutes.

In a large bowl, mix together the maple syrup, spices and salt flakes. Add the sweet potato and toss them in the spiced maple mixture, coating all over.

Spread the sweet potato back on the baking tray and roast for a further 12–15 minutes, until cooked through and caramelised.

To serve, place some rocket on a warm tortilla, then top with the roasted sweet potato and a tablespoon of the corn and bean salsa. Scatter over the goat's cheese, dollop with avocado crema and serve immediately, with lime wedges.

CHEESY DEEP-FRIED ZUCCHINI BLOSSOMS

VEGETARIAN & VEGAN

12 baby zucchini (courgettes), with blossoms attached

125 g (4½ oz) oaxaca cheese or mozzarella, shredded

rice bran oil, for deep-frying

75 g (½ cup) self-raising flour

¼ teaspoon cayenne pepper

¼ teaspoon chipotle chilli powder

¼ teaspoon fine sea salt

¼ teaspoon cracked black pepper

250 ml (1 cup) dark Mexican beer

salt flakes

TO SERVE

Guacamole (page 35)

12 warm Corn tortillas (page 15)

Pickled red onion (page 35)

fresh green jalapeno chilli slices

1 tablespoon black sesame seeds, toasted

coriander (cilantro) leaves or radish micro herbs

hot sauce (optional)

Gently open the zucchini flower petals and remove and discard the stamens. Carefully stuff the flowers with a tablespoon of the cheese, then close back up again.

In a large saucepan, heat enough rice bran oil for deep-frying to 175°C (345°F) over medium–high heat.

In a bowl, combine the flour, spices, salt and pepper. Pour in the beer and whisk together.

Dip a few stuffed zucchini blossoms into the beer batter, then carefully add to the hot oil and cook for 3–4 minutes, until golden brown. Drain on paper towel while you cook the remaining zucchini, and sprinkle with a little flaked sea salt.

To serve, spread some guacamole on a warm tortilla. Cut a zucchini (and its blossom) in half lengthways, and place on top of the guacamole. Top with pickled onion, jalapeno slices, a sprinkling of sesame seeds and coriander leaves or micro herbs. Serve immediately, with a dash of hot sauce, if desired.

NOTE

These tacos are also great served with Tomatillo salsa verde (page 28).

MEXICAN STREET CORN

3 corn cobs, husks and silks removed

100 g (3½ oz) cotija or feta, crumbled

½ large avocado, diced

1 fresh green jalapeno chilli, seeds removed, diced

½ cup roughly chopped coriander (cilantro)

LIME PAPRIKA CREMA

60 g (¼ cup) Mexican crema or sour cream

1 tablespoon mayonnaise

1 small garlic clove, minced

zest of 1 lime

juice of 2–3 limes (depending on how tangy you'd like it)

½ teaspoon smoked paprika

½ teaspoons chilli powder

¼ teaspoon ground cumin

TO SERVE

12 warm small blue corn tortillas

Pickled red onion (page 35)

chilli powder or Tajin

lime wedges

Heat a chargrill pan over medium–high heat or a barbecue grill to medium–high. Grill the corn cobs, turning occasionally, for 8–9 minutes, until charred and lightly cooked. Remove from the heat and set aside to cool.

When cool enough to handle, slice the corn kernels off the cobs and gently toss in a bowl with the crumbled cheese, avocado, jalapeno chilli and coriander.

Mix the lime paprika crema ingredients in a bowl, then pour the crema over the corn mixture and gently toss to combine. Season to taste with sea salt and black pepper.

To serve, pile some creamy corn on a warm tortilla and top with pickled onion. Sprinkle with a dusting of chilli powder or Tajin, and serve immediately, with a juicy lime wedge.

PRAWN DIABLO

36 large prawns (shrimp), peeled and deveined

60 g (2 oz) salted butter

1 teaspoon olive oil

DIABLO SAUCE

4 dried arbol chillies, stems and seeds removed

4 dried guajillo chillies, stems and seeds removed

2 large tomatoes, roughly chopped

½ onion, roughly chopped

3 garlic cloves, peeled

½ teaspoon fine sea salt

good pinch of chilli flakes

30 g (1 oz) salted butter

TO SERVE

Mexican red rice (page 21)

12 warm Corn tortillas (page 15)

Mexican crema or sour cream

coriander (cilantro) leaves

lime wedges

Start by making the diablo sauce. Place the dried chillies in a heatproof bowl, cover with boiling water and set aside for about 30 minutes to allow the chillies to soften and rehydrate.

Pour 60 ml (¼ cup) of the chilli soaking liquid into a blender. Drain the rehydrated chillies and add them to the blender, along with the tomatoes, onion, garlic, salt and chilli flakes, then blitz to a smooth consistency. You can use the sauce now, but if refrigerated overnight, the flavours will develop further.

To finish the sauce, melt the butter in a large frying pan over medium–low heat. Pour in the sauce and cook for about 4–5 minutes, to thicken the sauce slightly.

While the sauce is warming, butterfly the prawns. To do this, run a small sharp knife down along the back of the prawns, cutting deeply, but not all the way through the flesh. Lightly season the prawns with sea salt and black pepper.

Place a cast-iron frying pan over medium–high heat, add the butter and olive oil and allow to meld. Fry the prawns in batches for about 1 minute each side, until almost cooked through.

Gently toss the prawns and any residual juices through the diablo sauce, coating them thoroughly in the sauce.

To serve, spoon some Mexican red rice onto a warm tortilla. Top with three saucy prawns and a squiggle of crema. Scatter over some coriander and serve immediately, with lime wedges.

LOBSTER TAILS *with* LIME CHILLI BUTTER

6 small lobster tails, each about 120 g (4½ oz) with shell

LIME CHILLI BUTTER

150 g (5½ oz) butter, melted

zest and juice of 2 limes

2 garlic cloves, finely grated

2 tablespoons finely chopped coriander (cilantro)

1 tablespoon finely chopped chives

½ teaspoon chipotle chilli powder

TO SERVE

6 warm Flour tortillas (page 14)

Mango salsa (page 32)

coriander (cilantro) leaves

lime wedges

Blow-your-head-off habanero hot sauce (page 39, optional)

To make the lime chilli butter, place the ingredients in a bowl and whisk to combine.

Heat a barbecue grill to medium–high or place a chargrill pan over medium–high heat. Brush the flesh side of the lobster tails with the lime chilli butter, then place on the grill or in the pan, cut side down. Cook for 2–3 minutes, until the shells change colour.

Flip the tails over, brush on more lime chilli butter and cook for a further 2–3 minutes, until the lobster flesh turns opaque and is just cooked through.

To serve, remove the lobster flesh from each shell and cut in half. Place on a warm tortilla and top with mango salsa, coriander, a squeeze of lime juice and a drizzle of the remaining lime chilli butter. Serve immediately, with a splash of habanero hot sauce, if desired.

NOTE

These tacos are also delicious with Pineapple salsa (page 34), Roasted corn & black bean salsa (page 28) and Chipotle crema (page 145).

SPICY AHI POKE

SEAFOOD

oil, for shallow-frying

12 small Corn tortillas (page 15)

450 g (1 lb) sashimi-grade ahi tuna

1 Lebanese (short) cucumber, halved lengthways, seeds scraped out

1 avocado

½ small sweet salad onion, peeled and finely diced

1 teaspoon toasted black sesame seeds

1 teaspoon shichimi togarashi

SRIRACHA CREMA

125 g (½ cup) Mexican crema, sour cream or creme fraiche

2–3 teaspoons sriracha chilli sauce, or more to taste

SHOYU & GINGER MARINADE

2 tablespoons shoyu

1 tablespoon rice wine vinegar

2 teaspoons toasted sesame oil

2 teaspoons honey

1–2 teaspoons sriracha chilli sauce

1½ teaspoons finely grated ginger

1 garlic clove, finely grated

TO SERVE

tobiko (flying fish roe, available from Asian grocery stores)

shichimi togarashi

coriander (cilantro) leaves

lime wedges

To make the sriracha crema, mix the ingredients in a small bowl until well blended. Refrigerate in a clean airtight container until required. It will keep in the fridge for up to 5 days, and makes about 125 g (½ cup).

Pour 3 cm (1¼ inches) of oil into a wide frying pan and place over medium–high heat. Heat the oil to 175°C (345°F), then, working in batches, fry the tortillas for 1–2 minutes, until golden brown. Drain the tortillas on paper towels set over a wire cooling rack.

Cut the tuna, cucumber and avocado into 1 cm (½ inch) dice and place in a large bowl. Add the salad onion, sesame seeds and shichimi togarashi and gently fold to combine.

In a separate bowl, whisk together the shoyu and ginger marinade ingredients, then taste, and add more sriracha if desired. Pour the marinade over the tuna mixture and gently toss to combine.

To serve, place some poke mixture on a fried tortilla, drizzle with sriracha crema, then add a small teaspoon of tobiko and a sprinkling of shichimi togarashi. Top with coriander and serve immediately, with a squeeze of lime.

OYSTER PO'BOY

185 ml (¾ cup) buttermilk

1 egg

60 ml (¼ cup) hot sauce

1 teaspoon cayenne pepper

18 freshly shucked oysters

oil, for deep-frying

REMOULADE SAUCE

160 g (⅔ cup) mayonnaise

2 tablespoons each dijon mustard, freshly grated horseradish, chopped parsley and lemon juice

1 tablespoon Red chilli sauce (page 42)

½ red capsicum (bell pepper), chopped

½ teaspoon each sea salt and black pepper

SPICED PANKO

30 g (½) cup panko breadcrumbs

35 g (¼ cup) each cornmeal and plain (all-purpose) flour

1½ teaspoons each cayenne pepper and fine sea salt

½ teaspoon each chipotle chilli powder, garlic powder and chopped oregano leaves

1 teaspoon each onion powder, hot paprika and black pepper

TO SERVE

6 warm Corn tortillas (page 15)

150 g (2 cups) shredded white cabbage

1 spring onion (scallion), thinly sliced

finely chopped garlic chives

2 teaspoons baby capers

lemon wedges

To make the remoulade sauce, place the ingredients in a blender and blitz until smooth and creamy. Refrigerate in a clean airtight container until required. The sauce will keep for 4–5 days, and makes about 250 g (1 cup).

In a bowl, whisk together the buttermilk, egg, hot sauce and cayenne pepper until well combined. Add the oysters, then cover and refrigerate for 20–30 minutes.

Place the spiced panko ingredients in a bowl and stir well to combine.

In a large saucepan, heat enough oil for deep-frying to 175°C (345°F) over medium–high heat.

Remove the oysters from the buttermilk mixture, and toss to coat completely in the spiced panko.

Working in batches, carefully lower the oysters into the hot oil and fry for about 2 minutes, until golden brown and crispy. Remove and drain on paper towels set over a wire cooling rack, and sprinkle with flaked salt and black pepper.

To serve, place some remoulade sauce on a warm tortilla, then top with cabbage, a little spring onion and three oysters. Drizzle over some more remoulade, then finish with a sprinkling of garlic chives, baby capers and a squeeze of lemon. Serve immediately.

MOJO DE AJO SCALLOPS *with* CUCUMBER SALSA

SEAFOOD

12 large scallops

1 teaspoon olive oil

45 g (1½ oz) butter

2 garlic cloves, minced

zest and juice of ½ small lemon

good pinch of chilli flakes

CUCUMBER SALSA

200 g (1½ cups) finely diced cucumber

½ white onion, finely diced

1 fresh green jalapeno chilli, seeds removed, finely diced

large handful of coriander (cilantro) leaves, chopped

2 tablespoons lime juice

1 teaspoon finely grated lime zest

pinch of sea salt

TO SERVE

8 warm small blue corn tortillas

Avocado tomatillo sauce (page 32)

lime wedges

Combine the cucumber salsa ingredients in a glass bowl, then cover and refrigerate until ready to serve. (The salsa is best consumed on the day it is made.)

Pat the scallops dry with paper towel, then season both sides well with sea salt and black pepper.

Heat a cast-iron frying pan over medium–high heat. Add the olive oil and butter and allow to meld. Working in batches if needed, sear the scallops on one side for about 3½ minutes, until lightly browned with a golden crust. Flip them over, add the garlic and cook for 30 seconds.

Add the lemon zest, lemon juice and chilli flakes and continue to cook for a further 1–1½ minutes, basting the scallops with the buttery citrus garlic sauce.

To serve, place three scallops on a warm double-stacked blue corn tortilla. Add a spoonful of cucumber salsa, a splash of avocado tomatillo sauce and serve immediately, with lime wedges.

CEVICHE VERACRUZ

600 g (1 lb 5 oz) kingfish fillet, skin and bones removed, cut into 1 cm (½ inch) dice

½ small red onion, finely diced

½ cup finely chopped coriander (cilantro) leaves

1–2 fresh green jalapeno chillies, seeds removed, finely diced

60 ml (¼ cup) orange juice

125 ml (½ cup) lime juice

vegetable or rice bran oil, for shallow-frying

12 small Corn tortillas (page 15)

1 tomatillo, husk removed, rinsed and diced

1 small tomato, diced

1 avocado, cut into 1 cm (½ inch) dice

TO SERVE

40 g (1½ oz) watercress sprigs

4 heirloom or rainbow radishes, thinly sliced

micro herbs

extra virgin olive oil, for drizzling

Place the fish, onion, coriander, chilli and citrus juices in a glass bowl. Gently toss to combine, then cover and refrigerate for 1–2 hours.

Pour 3 cm (1¼ inches) of oil into a wide frying pan and place over medium–high heat. Heat the oil to 175°C (345°F), then, working in batches, fry the tortillas for 1–2 minutes, until golden brown. Drain the tortillas on paper towels set over a wire cooling rack.

Remove the fish from the fridge. Add the tomatillo, tomato and avocado and gently toss through, then season with sea salt flakes and black pepper.

To serve, place some watercress on a fried tortilla, then add some ceviche. Finish with a little sliced radish, a few micro herbs and a drizzle of olive oil. Serve immediately.

CHARGRILLED OCTOPUS with LEMON, CHILLI and GARLIC

2 bay leaves

½ teaspoon black peppercorns

I onion, peeled and quartered

I small orange, unpeeled, cut into quarters

900 g (2 lb) octopus tentacles, cleaned

LEMON, CHILLI & GARLIC MARINADE

170 ml (⅔ cup) extra virgin olive oil

zest and juice of 2 lemons

⅔ cup finely chopped coriander (cilantro) leaves

2–3 red bird's eye chillies, seeds removed, very finely chopped

5–6 large garlic cloves, crushed

TO SERVE

Guacamole (page 35)

18 warm Corn tortillas (page 15)

Pickled red onion (page 35)

I fresh green jalapeno chilli, thinly sliced

coriander (cilantro) leaves

lemon wedges

Place a large saucepan of water over high heat. Add the bay leaves, peppercorns, and onion and orange quarters and bring to the boil. Add the octopus tentacles, bring to the boil again, then reduce the heat to a simmer. Cover and braise the octopus for about 45 minutes, until the tentacles are tender when pierced with a knife.

While the octopus is braising, place the lemon, chilli and garlic marinade ingredients in a large bowl and whisk to combine. Remove one-quarter of the marinade and set aside.

Allow the octopus to cool in the cooking liquid, then remove to a chopping board. Cut the thickest part of the tentacles into 1 cm (½ inch) slices. Leave the thinnest end of the tentacles in long pieces.

Add the octopus pieces to the larger quantity of marinade and toss to coat. Cover and leave to marinate for 35–45 minutes at cool room temperature.

To char the octopus, heat a barbecue grill to medium–high or a chargrill pan over medium–high heat. Working in batches, cook the octopus for 2–3 minutes, turning occasionally, until the skin begins to blacken and char, while making sure that the flesh remains plump and juicy.

Place the octopus in a bowl and cover with the remaining marinade to soak up more flavour.

To serve, place some guacamole on a warm tortilla, then top with chargrilled octopus and some of the leftover marinade oil. Add a little pickled red onion, jalapeno chilli, coriander and a squeeze of lemon, and serve immediately.

NOTE

These tacos are also great with Pico de gallo (page 34), Green chilli sauce (page 43) or Blow-your-head-off habanero hot sauce (page 39).

HONEY–CHIPOTLE SALMON

SEAFOOD

4 salmon fillets, skin and bones removed, cut into 3 cm (1¼ inch) cubes

LIME CHIPOTLE MARINADE

3 chipotle chillies in adobo sauce, finely chopped, plus 3 tablespoons of the sauce

3 tablespoons olive oil

2 garlic cloves, minced

2½ tablespoons honey

2 tablespoons lime juice

¼ teaspoon chilli flakes

TO SERVE

shredded purple cabbage

8 warm Corn tortillas (page 15)

½ ripe papaya, diced

75 g (½ cup) crumbled feta

Avocado crema (page 60)

Chipotle mayo (page 122, optional)

coriander (cilantro) leaves

Preheat the oven to 200ºC (400ºF). Line a baking tray with baking paper.

Toss together the lime chipotle marinade ingredients in a bowl with a little sea salt and black pepper and mix until well combined. (Alternatively, blitz in a small blender until a sauce forms, then tip into a bowl.)

Gently toss the salmon cubes through the marinade, coating evenly. Spread the salmon on the baking tray and roast for 5–6 minutes.

Remove the tray from the oven and, using a spatula, turn the salmon cubes over. Roast for a further 6–7 minutes, until perfectly cooked through.

To serve, place a little shredded cabbage on a warm tortilla, then top with some salmon, papaya and feta. Drizzle with avocado crema and chipotle mayo (if using), then scatter over some coriander and serve immediately.

SWORDFISH *with* SPICY LIME CREMA

1 kg (2 lb 3 oz) swordfish steaks, skin removed, cut into 20 even pieces

30–45 g (1–1½ oz) salted butter

½ lemon

SPICY LIME CREMA

160 g (⅔ cup) Mexican crema or sour cream

2 tablespoons lime juice

zest of 1 lime

1 teaspoon sriracha chilli sauce

¾ teaspoon chilli powder

pinch of sea salt

LEMON GARLIC MARINADE

90 ml (3 fl oz) extra virgin olive oil

3 tablespoons lemon juice

2 garlic cloves, minced

½ teaspoon sea salt

½ teaspoon cracked black pepper

TO SERVE

shredded purple cabbage

10 warm Corn tortillas (page 15)

Pineapple salsa (page 34) or Mango salsa (page 32)

coriander (cilantro) leaves

lemon or lime wedges

Place the spicy lime crema ingredients in a bowl and whisk to combine. Cover and refrigerate until ready to use; the crema will keep in a sealed glass container in the fridge for about 4 days.

Place the lemon garlic marinade ingredients in a glass bowl and whisk to combine. Gently toss the swordfish through, coating all the pieces. Cover and set aside to marinate for 1 hour at cool room temperature.

Heat a large cast-iron frying pan over medium–high heat and add the butter. Working in batches, taking care not to crowd the pan, fry the swordfish pieces on one side for about 4 minutes, then flip them over and fry for a further 1 minute, until just cooked through. Transfer each batch to a tray, squeezing some lemon juice over, then some of the buttery juices from the pan once all the fish is cooked.

To serve, place a little cabbage on a warm tortilla and add two fish pieces. Spoon over a little of the garlicky pan juices. Drizzle with spicy lime crema, add a dollop of salsa and scatter over some coriander. Serve immediately, with lemon or lime wedges.

BAJA FISH

vegetable oil, for deep-frying

225 g (1½ cups) plain (all-purpose) flour

1 teaspoon chipotle chilli powder

1 teaspoon fine sea salt

½ teaspoon black pepper

250 ml (1 cup) Mexican beer

900 g (2 lb) firm white fish fillets, such as flathead or snapper, skin and bones removed, cut into 24 pieces about 3 cm (1¼ inches) wide

CABBAGE SLAW

300 g (4 cups) shredded red cabbage

2 spring onions (scallions), thinly sliced

¼ cup chopped coriander (cilantro) leaves

60 g (¼ cup) mayonnaise

60 g (¼ cup) Mexican crema, sour cream or creme fraiche

zest and juice of 1 lime

TO SERVE

12 warm Corn tortillas (page 15)

Pico de gallo (page 34, optional)

12 avocado slices

Chipotle crema (page 145)

3 radishes, thinly sliced

lime wedges

In a large saucepan, heat enough oil for deep-frying to 175°C (345°F).

Meanwhile, place 150 g (1 cup) of the flour in a large bowl. Mix the chilli powder, salt and pepper through, then whisk in the beer to combine.

Dust the fish in the remaining 75 g (½ cup) of flour.

Dip the fish into the beer batter, one piece at a time, then carefully lower 2–3 pieces of fish into the hot oil. Fry for about 2 minutes each side, until golden brown, crispy and cooked through. Remove and drain on paper towel set over a wire cooling rack and sprinkle with sea salt flakes. Repeat with the remaining fish pieces.

Place the cabbage slaw ingredients in a bowl and toss to combine. Season with salt and pepper to taste.

To serve, place some slaw on a warm tortilla and top with pico de gallo (if using) and an avocado slice. Add two pieces of fried fish and drizzle over some chipotle crema. Finish with a few slices of radish and a squeeze of lime. Serve immediately.

CHICKEN TAQUITOS

▲▲▲▲▲▲▲▲▲▲▲▲▲▲▲▲▲▲▲▲▲▲▲ CHICKEN, DUCK & TURKEY ▲▲▲▲▲▲▲▲▲▲▲▲▲▲▲▲▲▲▲▲▲▲▲

4 boneless chicken breasts, about 1 kg (2 lb 3 oz), skin removed

1 bay leaf

1 garlic clove, peeled and smashed

12 warm Corn tortillas (page 15)

vegetable or rice bran oil, for shallow-frying

TO SERVE

shredded iceberg lettuce

Avocado tomatillo sauce (page 32)

Mexican crema, sour cream or creme fraiche

crumbled cotija cheese or mild feta

coriander (cilantro) leaves

lime wedges

Place the chicken breasts in a saucepan with the bay leaf and garlic clove, then cover with cold water. Place over high heat, bring to the boil and cook for 1 minute. Cover with a tight-fitting lid and turn off the heat, then leave the chicken to slowly poach for 15–20 minutes. Remove from the heat.

Preheat the oven to very low.

When the chicken is cool enough to handle, shred the meat and season with sea salt and black pepper.

Fill a tortilla with a small amount of the shredded chicken, then roll up tightly and secure with a wooden toothpick to keep the chicken enclosed. Repeat until all the tortillas have been filled.

Pour 3 cm (1¼ inches) of oil into a wide frying pan and place over medium–high heat. Heat the oil to 175°C (345°F), then, working in batches, fry the taquitos, turning now and then, for 2–3 minutes, until golden brown and crispy on all sides. Remove to a wire rack set over a baking tray, and keep warm in the oven while you fry the remaining taquitos.

To serve, place some shredded lettuce on a plate, then top with two or three taquitos. Drizzle with avocado tomatillo sauce and crema. Scatter over some cheese, coriander and add a squeeze of lime, and serve immediately.

CHICKEN TINGA

4 boneless chicken breasts, about 1 kg (2 lb 3 oz), skin removed

1 bay leaf

1 garlic clove, peeled and smashed

TINGA SAUCE

2 teaspoons olive oil

1 large onion, diced

2 large garlic cloves, crushed

1 teaspoon dried Mexican oregano

1 teaspoon ground cumin

60 ml (¼ cup) reserved chicken poaching liquid

2 × 400 g (14 oz) tins diced tomatoes

4 chipotle chillies in adobo sauce, finely chopped, plus 2 tablespoons of the sauce

TO SERVE

Mexican crema, sour cream or creme fraiche

12 warm Corn tortillas (page 15)

crumbled queso anejo cheese or feta

3 radishes, thinly sliced

Pickled red onion (page 35)

fresh green jalapeno chilli slices

lime wedges

Place the chicken breasts in a saucepan with the bay leaf and garlic clove, then cover with cold water. Place over high heat, bring to the boil, and cook for 1 minute. Cover with a tight-fitting lid and turn off the heat, then leave the chicken to slowly poach for 15–20 minutes. Remove from the heat.

When the chicken is cool enough to handle, thinly shred the meat and set aside. Reserve 60 ml (¼ cup) of the chicken poaching liquid for the tinga sauce.

To make the tinga sauce, place the oil in a saucepan over medium heat, add the onion and saute for 5–7 minutes, until translucent and soft. Add the garlic, oregano and cumin and fry for a further minute. Stir in the reserved chicken poaching liquid, along with the tomatoes, chipotle chilli and adobo sauce. Add the shredded chicken and simmer for 8–10 minutes, until the sauce has thickened slightly. Season with sea salt and black pepper to taste.

To serve, drizzle some crema on a warm tortilla, then top with chicken tinga, cheese, radish and pickled onion. Finish with a few jalapeno chilli slices and a squeeze of lime. Serve immediately.

HAWAIIAN-STYLE HULI HULI CHICKEN

▲▲▲▲▲▲▲▲▲▲▲▲▲▲▲▲▲▲▲▲▲▲▲▲ CHICKEN, DUCK & TURKEY ▲▲▲▲▲▲▲▲▲▲▲▲▲▲▲▲▲▲▲▲▲▲▲▲

1 kg (2 lb 3 oz) boneless chicken thighs, skin removed

vegetable oil, for brushing

SWEET SOY & GINGER MARINADE

80 ml (⅓ cup) pineapple juice

80 ml (⅓ cup) soy sauce

80 g (⅓ cup) tomato ketchup

60 ml (¼ cup) sherry

60 g (¼ cup) brown sugar

3 tablespoons honey

1 tablespoon apple cider vinegar

1 tablespoon sriracha chilli sauce

1 tablespoon sesame oil

1 tablespoon minced ginger

2–3 garlic cloves, minced

TO SERVE

shredded purple cabbage

18 warm small Flour tortillas (page 14)

Pineapple salsa (page 34)

2 spring onions (scallions), thinly sliced

fresh green jalapeno chilli slices

lime wedges

Place the sweet soy and ginger marinade ingredients in a large glass bowl and whisk to combine. Remove about 125 ml (½ cup) of the marinade and reserve for basting. Add the chicken thighs to the remaining marinade and toss to coat, then cover and refrigerate for at least 4 hours, or overnight at the most. Bring to cool room temperature 30 minutes before grilling.

Heat a barbecue grill to medium–high and brush the grill plate with oil. (Alternatively, place a chargrill pan on the stovetop over medium–high heat and brush with oil.)

Remove the chicken from the marinade, discarding the marinade. Grill the chicken for 3 minutes on one side, then turn and grill for 3 minutes on the other side. Turn and grill for a further 2 minutes on each side, then turn again and grill for a further 1 minute on each side, basting with the reserved marinade all the while (huli huli means 'turn turn').

When the chicken is lightly charred, sticky and cooked through, transfer to a plate, lightly cover and leave to rest for 3–4 minutes, before slicing into strips.

To serve, place some shredded cabbage on a warm tortilla and add a few chicken strips. Top with a little pineapple salsa, spring onion and jalapeno. Serve immediately, with lime wedges.

STREET-STYLE CHICKEN *with* CHICKEN SKIN CHICHARRONES

▲▲▲▲▲▲▲▲▲▲▲▲▲▲▲▲▲▲▲▲▲▲ CHICKEN, DUCK & TURKEY ▲▲▲▲▲▲▲▲▲▲▲▲▲▲▲▲▲▲▲▲▲▲

500 g (1 lb 2 oz) boneless chicken thighs, skin on

olive oil, for brushing

HERB CITRUS MARINADE

3 tablespoons orange juice

3 tablespoons lime juice

3 tablespoons lemon juice

2 garlic cloves, minced

1 teaspoon sea salt

½ teaspoon cracked black pepper

½ teaspoon onion powder

½ teaspoon ground cumin

½ teaspoon dried oregano (not Mexican)

TO SERVE

6–8 warm small Corn tortillas (page 15)

1 small white onion, diced

coriander (cilantro) leaves, chopped

Red chilli sauce (page 42)

Tomatillo salsa verde (page 28)

lime wedges

Remove the chicken skin from the thighs and reserve for the chicharrones.

Mix the herb citrus marinade ingredients together in a large glass bowl. Add the chicken thighs and toss to coat, then cover and refrigerate for at least 2 hours, or overnight. Bring to cool room temperature 30 minutes prior to cooking.

Preheat the oven to 200ºC (400ºF). To make the chicharrones, pat the reserved chicken skin dry with paper towel. Place on a wire rack set over a baking tray and very lightly season with sea salt and black pepper. Transfer the tray to the oven and roast the chicken skin for 18–20 minutes, until golden brown and crispy. Remove from the oven and set aside.

Place a chargrill pan or cast-iron frying pan over medium–high heat and brush generously with oil. Remove the chicken thighs from the marinade, discarding the marinade. When the pan is hot, fry the chicken for 5–6 minutes on each side, until cooked through.

Transfer the chicken to a plate, lightly cover and leave to rest for 3–4 minutes, before slicing into strips.

To serve, place some chicken strips on a warm tortilla, then top with a little onion, coriander, chilli sauce and salsa. Crumble some chicken skin chicharrones over for a delicious crunchy topping and serve immediately, with lime wedges.

HARISSA CHICKEN *with* LEMONY LABNEH

500 g (1 lb 2 oz) boneless chicken thighs, skin on

olive oil, for brushing

LEMONY LABNEH

250 g (1 cup) labneh

1 tablespoon lemon juice

1 teaspoon lemon zest

ORANGE-HARISSA MARINADE

2½ tablespoons harissa paste

2 tablespoons honey

1 tablespoon olive oil

zest and juice of ½ orange

2–3 garlic cloves, minced

½ teaspoon sea salt

¼ teaspoon cracked black pepper

¼ teaspoon ground cinnamon

TO SERVE

6–8 warm Corn tortillas (page 15)

1 small avocado, sliced

Pickled red onion (page 35)

coriander (cilantro) leaves

lemon wedges

Place the lemony labneh ingredients in a bowl and mix to combine. The labneh will keep in a sealed glass container in the fridge for 5–7 days.

In a large bowl, whisk together the orange–harissa marinade ingredients. Add the chicken to the marinade, turning to coat thoroughly. Cover and refrigerate for at least 2 hours, or overnight at the most. Bring to cool room temperature 30 minutes prior to cooking.

Preheat the oven to 170°C (340°F).

Place a chargrill pan over high heat and brush with oil. Fry the chicken thighs for 5–6 minutes on each side, then transfer to a roasting tin and place in the oven. Roast for 5 minutes or until the chicken is cooked through.

Transfer the chicken to a plate, lightly cover and leave to rest for 3–4 minutes, before slicing into strips.

To serve, spread some lemony labneh on a warm tortilla, then add a few slices of chicken and avocado. Top with pickled red onion and coriander leaves and serve immediately, with lemon wedges.

DUCK *with* CHERRY *and* BLOOD ORANGE SALSA

4 duck breasts, skin on

CHERRY & BLOOD ORANGE SALSA

1 tablespoon diced shallot

180 g (6½ oz) cherries, pitted and sliced

125 ml (½ cup) blood orange juice

60 ml (¼ cup) Cointreau or other orange-flavoured liqueur

1 bay leaf

⅛ teaspoon white peppercorns, crushed

2 large blood oranges, segmented

TO SERVE

rocket (arugula) leaves

8 warm Corn tortillas (page 15)

Pickled red onion (page 35)

coriander (cilantro) leaves

Blow-your-head-off habanero hot sauce (page 39)

Preheat the oven to 190°C (375°F).

Rinse the duck breasts, pat dry with paper towel and season with sea salt and black pepper.

Place the duck breasts, skin side down, in a large ovenproof frying pan over medium heat. Cook for 2–3 minutes, until most of the fat has rendered out into the pan, then increase the heat and cook for a further 2–3 minutes, until the skin is crisp and golden brown.

Turn the duck over and cook for a further 2–3 minutes, then transfer the pan to the oven and bake for 7–8 minutes, to cook the duck through to medium.

Remove the duck from the oven, then transfer to a plate, keep warm and leave to rest for about 5 minutes.

To make the cherry and blood orange salsa, pour off most of the fat from the pan, then place back over medium heat. Add the shallot, cherries and blood orange juice and cook for 2–3 minutes. Stir in the Cointreau, bay leaf and crushed white peppercorns and cook for 2–3 minutes, until the sauce has reduced slightly. Remove from the heat and toss the orange segments through the sauce.

To serve, cut the duck breasts into 5 mm (¼ inch) thick slices. Place some rocket on a warm tortilla, then top with some duck slices and salsa. Finish with pickled red onion, coriander and a little habanero hot sauce. Serve immediately.

NOTE

Instead of the cherry and blood orange salsa, these tacos are also great with Mango salsa (page 32) or Pineapple salsa (page 34).

TURKEY *with* JACK CHEESE *and* PICKLED ONION

2 tablespoons olive oil

I onion, diced

I fresh poblano chilli, seeds removed, diced

1½ tablespoons Taco seasoning (see recipe below)

I kg (2 lb 3 oz) minced (ground) turkey

185 ml (¾ cup) tomato sugo

2 chipotle chillies in adobo sauce, chopped, plus 2 tablespoons of the adobo sauce

TACO SEASONING

I tablespoon chilli powder

1½ teaspoons ground cumin

1½ teaspoons smoked paprika

½ teaspoon onion powder

½ teaspoon garlic powder

½ teaspoon dried oregano (not Mexican)

½ teaspoon chilli flakes

I teaspoon fine sea salt

I teaspoon cracked black pepper

TO SERVE

20 warm Corn tortillas (page I5)

shredded Monterey jack cheese

Pickled red onion (page 35)

Avocado tomatillo sauce (page 32) or Red chilli sauce (page 42)

Mexican crema or sour cream

lime wedges dipped in Tajin

Measure all the taco seasoning ingredients into a glass jar. Seal the jar and shake to combine. You'll have more than you need for this recipe, but the left-over spice mix will keep in the pantry for 2–3 months.

Heat the olive oil in a large frying pan over medium heat. Saute the onion and poblano chilli for about 5 minutes, until they begin to soften. Add the taco seasoning, then crumble in the turkey. Cook for 7–8 minutes, stirring with a wooden spoon to break up the meat, until lightly browned.

Add the sugo to the pan, along with the chopped chipotle chillies and adobo sauce. Stir through and allow to simmer for about 4 minutes, until the sauce thickens slightly. Season to taste with sea salt and black pepper.

To serve, spread some saucy turkey meat on a warm tortilla and top with cheese and pickled red onion. Drizzle your chosen sauce over and add a dollop of crema. Serve immediately, with Tajin-dipped lime wedges.

KARAAGE-STYLE CHICKEN

4 boneless chicken thighs, skin on, cut into 5 cm (2 inch) pieces

160 g (1 cup) potato starch

½ teaspoon sea salt

½ teaspoon cracked black pepper

vegetable or rice bran oil, for deep-frying

TAMARI & GINGER MARINADE

4 garlic cloves, finely grated

20 g (¾ oz) piece of ginger, peeled and finely grated

60 ml (¼ cup) tamari

60 ml (¼ cup) sweet sake

2 teaspoons toasted sesame oil

1 teaspoon sriracha chilli sauce

½ teaspoon shichimi togarashi

SPICY SLAW

150 g (2 cups) shredded purple cabbage

90 g (1 cup) bean sprouts

60 g (¼ cup) kewpie mayonnaise

1 tablespoon sweet chilli sauce

TO SERVE

8 warm Corn tortillas (page 15)

sriracha chilli sauce

coriander (cilantro) leaves

1 teaspoon toasted black sesame seeds

Place the tamari and ginger marinade ingredients in a large glass bowl and whisk to combine. Add the chicken and stir through to coat, then cover and refrigerate for 30 minutes.

To make the spicy slaw, combine the ingredients in a mixing bowl and toss to combine. Cover and refrigerate until required.

Combine the potato starch, salt and pepper in a bowl. Remove the chicken from the fridge; drain and discard the marinade.

In a large saucepan, heat enough oil for deep-frying to 170°C (340°F). Toss the chicken in the potato starch, coating thoroughly. Fry the chicken in batches for 3 minutes, or until almost cooked through, then drain on a wire cooling rack set over paper towels.

Increase the heat to 190°C (375°F). Fry the chicken again, in batches, for 30–60 seconds, until golden brown and cooked through.

To serve, place some spicy slaw on a warm tortilla and top with a few pieces of chicken. Serve immediately, drizzled with sriracha, and garnished with coriander leaves and sesame seeds.

FAJITA-STYLE CHICKEN

3 boneless chicken breasts, about 750 g (1 lb 11 oz), skin removed

1 red capsicum (bell pepper), sliced

1 yellow capsicum (bell pepper), sliced

1 large red onion, sliced

LIME, CORIANDER & CHILLI MARINADE

½ cup chopped coriander (cilantro)

125 ml (½ cup) olive oil

60 ml (¼ cup) lime juice

2 garlic cloves, crushed

1½ teaspoons ground cumin

1½ teaspoons ancho chilli powder

½ teaspoon sea salt

½ teaspoon cracked black pepper

TO SERVE

12 warm Flour tortillas (page 14)

Guacamole (page 35)

Mexican crema, sour cream or creme fraiche

Fresh tomato salsa (page 30)

Place the lime, coriander and chilli marinade ingredients in a large glass bowl and whisk to combine. Add the chicken breasts, capsicums and onion, tossing to coat in the marinade. Cover and refrigerate for 30 minutes.

Heat a chargrill pan over high heat and cook the chicken breasts for about 5–7 minutes on each side, until cooked through. Remove, keep warm and set aside to rest.

Grill the capsicums and onion, turning often, for 10–12 minutes, until tender and slightly charred.

Slice the chicken into strips. To serve, place some chicken on a warm tortilla. Add some grilled vegetables, then top with guacamole, crema and tomato salsa. Serve immediately.

BARBECUE SPICE–RUBBED CHICKEN

2½ tablespoons olive oil

3 boneless chicken breasts, about 750 g (1 lb 11 oz), skin removed

6 spring onions (scallions), roots trimmed

BARBECUE SPICE RUB

1 tablespoon panela (see Note) or brown sugar

2 teaspoons ground cumin

2 teaspoons ancho chilli powder

2 teaspoons smoked paprika

1½ teaspoons ground coriander

1 teaspoon cayenne pepper

1 teaspoon ground cinnamon

1 teaspoon garlic powder

1 teaspoon onion powder

1 teaspoon fine sea salt

½ teaspoon cracked black pepper

TO SERVE

Roasted tomato salsa (page 31)

12 warm Corn tortillas (page 15)

pickled jalapeno chilli slices

Red chilli sauce (page 42)

lime wedges

chopped coriander (cilantro) leaves

Place the barbecue spice rub ingredients in a large glass bowl and stir to combine.

Stir through 2 tablespoons of the olive oil, then add the chicken breasts, tossing to coat them in the spice rub thoroughly. Set aside for 15 minutes to marinate.

Heat a chargrill pan over high heat and cook the chicken breasts for 5–7 minutes on each side, until cooked through. Transfer the chicken to a plate, keep warm and rest for 3–4 minutes before slicing.

Meanwhile, toss the spring onions in the remaining oil, add to the chargrill pan and cook for 2–3 minutes, until lightly charred and cooked through. Slice the spring onions into quarters.

To serve, place a little tomato salsa on a warm tortilla. Top with some sliced chicken, two spring onion quarters, a few pickled jalapeno slices, some chilli sauce and more salsa. Squeeze over a lime wedge, scatter over some coriander and serve immediately.

NOTE

Panela is an unrefined cane sugar, typically used in Latin American recipes.

CARNITAS

500 g (1 lb 2 oz) lard

1 kg (2 lb 3 oz) boneless pork shoulder, cut into 5–6 cm (2–2½ inch) dice

1½ tablespoons panela (see Note) or brown sugar

1 tablespoon sea salt flakes

1 tablespoon ancho chilli powder

4 garlic cloves, peeled and smashed

1 small onion, peeled and quartered

1 orange, unpeeled, cut into quarters

1 bay leaf

1 cinnamon stick

TO SERVE

12 warm Corn tortillas (page 15)

1 small onion, diced

Fresh tomatillo salsa verde (page 28)

chopped coriander (cilantro) leaves

lime wedges

Preheat the oven to 145°C (295°F).

Melt the lard in a large flameproof casserole dish (Dutch oven) over medium heat. While it is melting, toss the pork cubes in a large bowl with the sugar, salt and chilli powder, coating completely and evenly. Place the seasoned pork into the melted lard with the remaining ingredients, then increase the heat and bring just to the boil.

Remove the dish from the heat, put the lid on and transfer to the oven. Cook for 2½–3 hours, until the pork is cooked through and fork tender.

Remove the pork from the lard mixture. When cool enough to handle, shred the meat, using two forks to pull it apart.

Serve the shredded pork immediately on warm tortillas, topped with onion, salsa verde, coriander and a squeeze of lime.

If not serving immediately, save some of the lard to use when reheating the pork: place a tablespoon of lard in a frying pan over high heat, add some shredded pork and fry until crispy and browned.

NOTE

Panela is an unrefined cane sugar, typically used in Latin American recipes.

CHILORIO

1.5 kg (3 lb 5 oz) boneless pork shoulder, cut into 4 pieces

2 bay leaves

10 black peppercorns

2 tablespoons lard or olive oil

CHILORIO ADOBO SAUCE

2 dried guajillo chillies, stems and seeds removed

4 dried ancho chillies, stems and seeds removed

6 garlic cloves, peeled

2 teaspoons ground cumin

2 teaspoons dried Mexican oregano

¼ teaspoon ground allspice

125 ml (½ cup) white vinegar

zest of 1 large orange

80 ml (⅓ cup) orange juice

1 teaspoon cracked black pepper

1½ teaspoons sea salt

TO SERVE

24 warm Corn tortillas (page 15)

Pickled red onion (page 35), or diced white onion

crumbled queso fresco or mild feta

chopped coriander (cilantro) leaves

Chipotle crema (page 145)

lime wedges

Place the pork in a large saucepan, cover with water and add the bay leaves and peppercorns. Bring to the boil over medium–high heat, then reduce the heat to low, cover and simmer for 2½–3 hours, until the pork is fork tender. Allow to cool, then shred the meat using two forks.

To make the chilorio adobo sauce, place the dried chillies in a bowl, cover with boiling water and set aside for 20 minutes to rehydrate. When softened, add 185 ml (¾ cup) of the chilli soaking water to a blender. Add the softened chillies and the remaining sauce ingredients. Process to a smooth paste.

Add the lard or olive oil to a large saucepan over medium heat and warm through. Carefully add the chilorio adobo sauce, as it may splatter, and cook for 7–10 minutes, until reduced slightly. Add the shredded pork and stir it through, coating the meat in the sauce. Taste and adjust the seasoning, adding more salt if needed. Cook for a further 10–15 minutes, until the meat has absorbed all of the sauce.

To serve, place some chilorio on a double-stacked warm tortilla, then top with pickled onion, crumbled cheese, coriander and a drizzle of chipotle crema. Finish with a squeeze of lime and serve immediately.

SPICY ITALIAN SAUSAGE *with* BURRATA *and* SALSA VERDE

1 tablespoon olive oil

450 g (1 lb) Italian-style chilli and fennel pork sausages, casings removed

2 roma (plum) tomatoes, diced

60 g (¼ cup) tomato paste (concentrated puree)

125 ml (½ cup) white wine (or water)

ITALIAN SALSA VERDE

large handful of parsley leaves

large handful of basil leaves

80 ml (⅓ cup) extra virgin olive oil

2 garlic cloves

2 white anchovy fillets (in oil)

2 tablespoons lemon juice

2 teaspoons salt-packed baby capers, well rinsed

1 teaspoon chopped oregano leaves

½ teaspoon chopped rosemary leaves

½ teaspoon thyme leaves

TO SERVE

8 warm small Corn tortillas (page 15)

2 balls of burrata or buffalo mozzarella

diced Calabrian chilli

Place the Italian salsa verde ingredients in a blender and blitz until well combined, but not entirely smooth. Season with black pepper to taste. The salsa verde will keep in a sealed glass container in the fridge for about 5 days.

Warm a frying pan over medium–high heat and add the olive oil. Crumble the sausage meat into the pan and, using a wooden spoon, break it up into smaller pieces as it browns. Cook for 5–6 minutes, until almost cooked through.

Stir the diced tomatoes through the sausage meat and cook for a further 2 minutes. Stir in the tomato paste and wine, then cook for a few more minutes, until the sauce has reduced slightly. Season to taste with sea salt and black pepper.

To serve, place a tablespoon of the spicy sausage mixture on a warm tortilla. Add a few pieces of torn burrata. Drizzle with salsa verde, top with a little chilli and serve immediately.

CHORIZO, POTATO *and* FRIED EGG

◆◆◆◆◆◆◆◆◆◆◆◆◆◆◆◆◆◆◆◆◆◆◆◆◆◆◆◆◆ PORK ◆◆◆◆◆◆◆◆◆◆◆◆◆◆◆◆◆◆◆◆◆◆◆◆◆◆◆◆◆◆

1 large potato, scrubbed but not peeled, cut into 2 cm (¾ inch) dice

3 tablespoons olive oil

½ teaspoon smoked paprika

400 g (14 oz) Mexican chorizo sausages, casings removed

1 small onion, diced

40 g (1½ oz) butter

8 small organic free-range eggs

1 teaspoon chilli flakes

TO SERVE

Refried beans (page 19)

8 warm Corn tortillas (page 15)

shredded cheese of your choice

Roasted tomato salsa (page 31) or Roasted tomatillo salsa verde (page 28)

Mexican crema, sour cream or creme fraiche

Red chilli sauce (page 42)

coriander (cilantro) leaves

Mexican red rice (page 21)

Place the potato in a small saucepan of water and bring to the boil over high heat. Reduce the heat to a high simmer, then cook for 4 minutes or until soft and cooked through. Drain and set aside.

Heat 1 tablespoon of the oil in a frying pan over medium–high heat. Add the potato and paprika, season with sea salt and black pepper and cook, stirring frequently, for 5–6 minutes, until golden brown and crispy. Remove from the pan and keep warm.

Crumble the chorizo sausages into the same pan, add the onion and, using a wooden spoon, saute over medium–high heat for 5–7 minutes, until the chorizo is cooked through and the onion is soft and translucent. Combine with the potato, and keep warm while frying the eggs.

In a frying pan large enough to hold all the eggs, heat the remaining 2 tablespoons of oil and the butter over medium heat. When the oil is warm and the butter has melted, crack the eggs into the pan. Increase the heat to get the egg whites sizzling, then cook for 2–3 minutes, until all the whites are just cooked through and firm. Season with sea salt, black pepper and the chilli flakes.

To serve, place a tablespoon of refried beans on a warm tortilla, then top with some chorizo mixture and cheese. Add an egg, some salsa, a dollop of crema and chilli sauce, and some coriander to finish. Serve immediately, with Mexican red rice on the side.

PORK CHILLI VERDE

60 ml (¼ cup) olive oil

1 kg (2 lb 3 oz) boneless pork shoulder, cut into 4 cm (1½ inch) dice

1 teaspoon sea salt

1 teaspoon cracked black pepper

1½ teaspoons ground cumin

1½ teaspoons ground coriander

1 bay leaf

½ cup chopped coriander (cilantro) leaves

VERDE SAUCE

1 large onion, quartered

4 fresh poblano chillies, halved, stems and seeds removed

4 fresh green jalapeno chillies, halved, stems and half the seeds removed

500 g (1 lb 2 oz) tomatillos, husks removed, rinsed

4 large garlic cloves, peeled

1½ teaspoons dried Mexican oregano

500 ml (2 cups) chicken stock

TO SERVE

24 warm Corn tortillas (see Note; page 15)

crumbled queso fresco or mild feta

chopped coriander (cilantro) leaves

lime wedges

Mexican red rice (page 21)

Black beans in the pot (page 18)

Heat an oven grill (broiler) to medium–high. To make the verde sauce, place the onion, chillies, tomatillos and garlic cloves on a baking tray and grill (broil) for 10–15 minutes, turning once, until softened and lightly charred. Remove and set aside, placing the chillies in a bowl and covering with plastic wrap to steam for 10 minutes. Peel and discard the skin from the chillies. Place the chillies in a blender with the onion, tomatillos and garlic, add the remaining sauce ingredients and blitz until pureed. Set aside.

Heat the olive oil in a large flameproof casserole dish (Dutch oven) over medium–high heat. Sear the pork, in batches, for 4–5 minutes, until well browned, removing each batch to a plate.

Return all the pork to the dish. Add the salt, pepper, ground spices and bay leaf and pour in most of the verde sauce, stirring well. Bring the mixture to the boil, then cover, reduce the heat to low and simmer for 2½–3 hours, until the pork is tender and the sauce has reduced.

Just before serving, stir the coriander leaves through the pork mixture.

To serve, stack two warm tortillas on top of each other, to make a double layer. Top with some pork chilli verde, cheese, coriander and a squeeze of lime. Serve immediately, with red rice and beans, spooning the remaining verde sauce over the rice.

NOTE

Tacos with a wet stew-like filling ('guisado'), such as these ones, often use two tortillas instead of a single tortilla as a base.

SONORA DOGS

8 hot dogs

8 streaky bacon slices

CHIPOTLE MAYO

125 g (½ cup) mayonnaise

1 large chipotle chilli in adobo sauce

3 tablespoons lime juice

2 tablespoons sour cream

pinch of sea salt

TO SERVE

Beans in the pot (page 18)

8 warm Flour tortillas (page 14)

Pico de gallo (page 34)

hot sauce

whole pickled chillies (optional)

Place the chipotle mayo ingredients in a blender and blitz until smooth. The mayo will keep in a sealed glass container in the fridge for 5–7 days.

Wrap each hot dog with a slice of bacon. Tuck in the ends of the bacon, or secure with toothpicks, to stop the bacon unravelling during cooking.

Heat a large cast-iron frying pan or flat griddle over medium heat. Cook the bacon-wrapped hot dogs for 10–12 minutes, turning often, to ensure all sides are cooked, the bacon is browned and crisp, and the hot dogs are warmed through thoroughly.

Remove the toothpicks from the hot dogs, if you've used them. Spoon some beans on a warm tortilla, top with a bacon-wrapped hot dog and scatter over some pico de gallo. Drizzle with chipotle mayo and a splash of hot sauce and serve immediately, with whole pickled chillies, if desired.

BANH MI-STYLE PORK BELLY

PORK

2 tablespoons sea salt

1 teaspoon cracked black pepper

1 teaspoon cracked white pepper

1.2 kg (2 lb 10 oz) pork belly, skin on and scored (ask your butcher to do this), refrigerated overnight, uncovered

QUICK PICKLE CABBAGE SLAW

125 ml (½ cup) white vinegar

110 g (½ cup) white sugar

1 teaspoon sea salt

75 g (1 cup) shredded white cabbage

1 small carrot, julienned

1 small Lebanese (short) cucumber, julienned

½ small red onion, thinly sliced

1 red bird's eye chilli, thinly sliced

SWEET GLAZE

2 tablespoons kecap manis

2 tablespoons honey

1 tablespoon brown sugar

60 ml (¼ cup) soy sauce

2 tablespoons chopped coriander (cilantro)

TO SERVE

125 g (4½ oz) chicken liver pate

12 warm Flour tortillas (page 14)

kewpie mayonnaise

coriander (cilantro) leaves

thinly sliced red bird's eye chilli

Preheat the oven to 220°C (430°F).

Mix together the salt and black and white peppers, then rub the mixture all over the pork. Place the pork on a wire rack set over a baking tray, then roast in the oven for 30 minutes.

Reduce the oven temperature to 170°C (340°F) and roast the pork for a further 1–1½ hours, until the pork is tender and cooked through, and the skin is crisp. Remove from the oven and rest for 20–25 minutes.

Meanwhile, to make the quick pickle cabbage slaw, combine the vinegar, sugar and salt in a saucepan over low heat and stir to dissolve. Remove from the heat and allow to cool.

Combine the remaining slaw ingredients in a bowl, then pour over the cooled pickling liquid and mix well to combine. Cover and refrigerate for 30 minutes before using; the slaw will keep in a clean airtight container in the fridge for up to 2 days.

Slice the rested pork into 36 equal pieces. Mix together the sweet glaze ingredients, then brush all over the flesh of the pork.

Place a frying pan over medium–high heat and sear the glazed meat for 10–15 seconds on each side, until sticky and caramelised.

To serve, spread some chicken liver pate on a warm tortilla, then top with some slaw and glazed pork. Drizzle with mayonnaise, top with coriander leaves and chilli and serve immediately.

YUCATÁN 'COCHINITA PIBIL'

◆◆◆◆◆◆◆◆◆◆◆◆◆◆◆◆◆◆◆◆◆◆◆◆◆◆ PORK ◆◆◆◆◆◆◆◆◆◆◆◆◆◆◆◆◆◆◆◆◆◆◆◆◆◆

1.5 kg (3 lb 5 oz) boneless pork shoulder, cut into 6 pieces

1 tablespoon sea salt

banana leaves (see Notes), for lining

1 large onion, sliced

ACHIOTE MARINADE

½ cinnamon stick

2 cloves

1½ teaspoons cumin seeds

10 roasted garlic cloves, peeled

75 g (2¾ oz) achiote paste (see Notes)

1 teaspoon each ancho chilli powder, dried Mexican oregano and black pepper

125 ml (½ cup) orange juice

60 ml (¼ cup) lime juice

ROASTED TOMATO COOKING SAUCE

400 g (14 oz) tomatoes

4 garlic cloves, unpeeled

1 fresh red jalapeno chilli, stem removed

¼ cup chopped coriander (cilantro)

80 ml (⅓ cup) orange juice

2 tablespoons lime juice

1 teaspoon each sea salt and pepper

TO SERVE

12 warm Corn tortillas (page 15)

Pickled red onion (page 35)

sliced habanero chilli

sliced coriander (cilantro) leaves

Blow-your-head-off habanero hot sauce (page 39)

lime wedges

Rub the pork all over with the salt, then place in a large bowl and set aside.

To make the achiote marinade, toast the cinnamon stick, cloves and cumin seeds in a dry frying pan over medium heat, until fragrant. Transfer to a spice grinder and blitz to a powder. Place the spice powder and the remaining marinade ingredients in a blender and blitz to combine. Pour the marinade over the pork, turning to coat completely. Cover and marinate in the fridge for 4 hours, or preferably overnight.

Preheat the oven to 150°C (300°F).

To make the roasted tomato cooking sauce, place a cast-iron frying pan or chargrill pan over high heat and add the tomatoes, garlic and chilli. Roast the garlic, turning occasionally, for 6–7 minutes, and the tomatoes and chilli for 12–14 minutes, until blackened, charred and softly roasted.

Allow to cool, then peel the garlic and add to a blender with the tomatoes, chilli and remaining cooking sauce ingredients. Blitz to a puree.

Line a large flameproof casserole dish (Dutch oven) with banana leaves. Add the pork, then cover with the cooking sauce and scatter the onion slices over the top. Fold the banana leaves over the onion, covering the pork completely. Cover with a tight-fitting lid, transfer to the oven and cook for 3–3½ hours, until the meat is very tender.

Remove the dish from the oven and set aside until the pork is cool enough to handle. Remove and discard the banana leaves, then shred the meat using two forks. Return the pork to the dish and warm it through in the cooking sauce over low heat.

To serve, place some pork on a warm tortilla, then top with pickled red onion, habanero chilli, coriander and a splash of hot sauce. Add a squeeze of lime and serve immediately.

NOTES

Banana leaves are available from Asian grocery stores.

Achiote paste is a Yucatán ingredient made with bright-red annatto seeds, tomatoes and spices. You'll find it in Latin American grocery stores and online.

CHORIZO *and* QUESO FUNDIDÓ TACOS

PORK

I teaspoon olive oil

350 g (12½ oz) Mexican chorizo sausages, casings removed

I fresh poblano chilli, stem and seeds removed, diced

450 g (I lb) oaxaca cheese or mozzarella, shredded (see Note)

100 g (3½ oz) goat's cheese, crumbled

I fresh green jalapeno chilli, diced

small handful of coriander (cilantro) leaves

TO SERVE

12–14 warm Corn tortillas (page 15)

I small white onion, diced

Red chilli sauce (page 42)

Roasted tomato salsa (page 31)

Tomatillo salsa verde (page 28)

Preheat the oven to 180ºC (350ºF).

Place a 25 cm (10 inch) ovenproof cast-iron frying pan over medium–high heat and drizzle in the olive oil. Crumble in the chorizo and cook for about 2 minutes, stirring and breaking up the chorizo with a wooden spoon.

Add the poblano chilli and cook for a further 6–7 minutes, until the chorizo has cooked through and the chilli has softened slightly.

Drain and discard the excess oil from the pan, leaving the chorizo and chilli in the pan. Sprinkle the shredded cheese over the chorizo mixture, then transfer to the oven and bake for 10–12 minutes, until the cheese has melted and is bubbling and gooey.

Carefully remove the pan from the oven. Crumble the goat's cheese over, then top with the jalapeno and coriander.

To serve, scoop a large tablespoon of the cheese and chorizo mixture onto a warm tortilla. Sprinkle with a little diced onion, spoon over some chilli sauce and the salsas, and serve immediately.

NOTE

For a lovely smoky flavour, replace half the cheese with smoked scamorza, a pear-shaped Italian cheese similar to mozzarella.

'NDUJA SAUSAGE and SCRAMBLED EGG

PORK

8 large organic free-range eggs

60 ml (¼ cup) cream

30 g (1 oz) butter

2 teaspoons olive oil

8 sun-dried tomatoes, diced

TO SERVE

250 g (9 oz) 'nduja sausage (see Note)

8 warm Flour tortillas (page 14)

200 g (7 oz) fior di latte or buffalo mozzarella, torn

Red chilli sauce (page 42) or Calabrian chilli sauce

Tomatillo salsa verde (page 28)

6 small Chicharrones (page 24), or store-bought pork rinds, roughly crushed

Crack the eggs into a large bowl and whisk together. Add the cream and a good pinch of sea salt and black pepper and whisk again until fully combined.

Place a large frying pan over medium heat. Add the butter and olive oil and allow to melt and meld together.

Pour in the egg mixture and scatter the sun-dried tomatoes over. Use a wooden spoon to gently stir the egg while it cooks; you want it to remain creamy and soft, so reduce the heat to low if it's cooking too quickly.

To serve, spread some 'nduja over a warm tortilla, then add a tablespoon of the creamy scrambled egg. Top with a little cheese, chilli sauce and salsa verde. Finish with crushed chicharrones for a little crunch, and serve immediately.

NOTE

'Nduja is a spicy spreadable pork paste sausage from Calabria in southern Italy that requires no cooking. You'll find it in Mediterranean delicatessens and grocery stores.

GRILLED CARNE ASADA

1 kg (2 lb 3 oz) skirt steak

LIME, LEMON & CHIPOTLE MARINADE

80 ml (⅓ cup) olive oil

1 large onion, thinly sliced

4 garlic cloves, crushed

60 ml (¼ cup) lime juice

60 ml (¼ cup) lemon juice

1 tablespoon ground cumin

1 tablespoon chipotle chilli powder

2½ teaspoons cracked black pepper

1 teaspoon sea salt

TO SERVE

12 warm Corn tortillas (page 15)

Pico de gallo (page 34)

2 avocados, sliced

pickled jalapeno chilli slices

chopped coriander (cilantro)

lime wedges

Place the lime, lemon and chipotle marinade ingredients in a large glass bowl and whisk together. Add the steak, toss to coat, then cover and refrigerate for 3–4 hours, or overnight.

When ready to serve, heat a cast-iron frying pan or chargrill pan over medium heat. Add the steak and cook for 6–7 minutes, turning once. Allow to rest for 4–5 minutes, then slice the steak into strips.

To serve, place some steak on a warm tortilla. Top with pico de gallo, avocado slices, pickled jalapeno, coriander and a squeeze of lime. Serve immediately.

CUBAN BEEF PICADILLO

60 ml (¼ cup) olive oil

500 g (1 lb 2 oz) minced (ground) beef

1 potato, peeled and cut into 1 cm (½ inch) dice

1 carrot, cut into 1 cm (½ inch) dice

1 onion, thinly sliced

4 garlic cloves, crushed

1 tablespoon ground cumin

2 teaspoons smoked paprika

2 teaspoons mild chilli powder

1 teaspoon cracked black pepper

375 g (1½ cups) tomato passata (pureed tomatoes)

80 ml (⅓ cup) white vinegar

85 g (½ cup) pimento-stuffed whole green olives

40 g (⅓ cup) sultanas (golden raisins)

3 tablespoons baby capers, drained

1 teaspoon sea salt, or to taste

TO SERVE

shredded iceberg lettuce

12 warm Flour tortillas (page 14), about 15 cm (6 inches) in size

shredded cheese, such as oaxaca, mozzarella or cheddar

thinly sliced avocado

Mexican crema, sour cream or creme fraiche

Pickled taqueria-style vegetables (page 38)

Place a large frying pan over medium heat and add the olive oil. Add the beef and cook, breaking up any lumps with a wooden spoon, for about 5 minutes, until lightly browned. Stir in the potato and carrot and cook for 3–4 minutes, then add the onion and cook for a further 4 minutes. Stir in the garlic and spices and saute for 1–2 minutes, then add the remaining ingredients. Cook at a medium–low simmer for 20 minutes, stirring occasionally.

To serve, place some shredded lettuce on a warm tortilla, top with a tablespoon of beef picadillo, then some cheese, avocado and a drizzle of crema. Serve immediately, with pickled vegetables on the side.

KOFTAS *with* HARISSA YOGHURT *and* WHIPPED FETA

▼▼▼▼▼▼▼▼▼▼▼▼▼▼▼▼▼▼▼▼▼▼▼▼ BEEF & LAMB ▼▼▼▼▼▼▼▼▼▼▼▼▼▼▼▼▼▼▼▼▼▼▼▼

olive oil, for oiling and brushing

HARISSA YOGHURT

250 g (1 cup) Greek-style yoghurt

1 teaspoon harissa paste

1 teaspoon lemon juice

WHIPPED FETA

200 g (7 oz) Persian feta, drained

2 tablespoons Greek-style yoghurt

1 garlic clove, minced

½ teaspoon lemon zest

good pinch of Aleppo chilli flakes

KOFTAS

600 g (1 lb 5 oz) minced (ground) lamb

200 g (7 oz) minced (ground) beef (with 20% fat)

1 onion, grated

4 garlic cloves, minced

¼ cup chopped parsley

¼ cup chopped mint leaves

1½ teaspoons Aleppo chilli flakes

1½ teaspoons ground cumin

1 teaspoon fine sea salt

1 teaspoon cracked black pepper

1 teaspoon ground sumac

½ teaspoon ground cinnamon

TO SERVE

12 warm small Flour tortillas (page 14)

mint and coriander (cilantro) leaves

small handful of chopped pistachios

pomegranate molasses, for drizzling

lemon wedges

Place the harissa yoghurt ingredients in a bowl and whisk well to combine; taste and add a little more harissa paste if you'd like a bit more heat.

Place the whipped feta ingredients in a food processor and blitz until smooth and creamy. The harissa yoghurt and whipped feta will keep in separate airtight glass containers in the fridge for up to 5 days.

Place the kofta ingredients in a large mixing bowl and combine well. Using lightly oiled hands, divide the mixture into 24 even pieces, about 40 g (1½ oz) each. Shape into koftas about 8 cm (3¼ inches) long and 1.5 cm (½ inch) thick.

Place a chargrill pan over medium–high heat and brush with a little oil. Working in batches, cook the koftas, turning occasionally, for 7–9 minutes, until well browned all over, and cooked through.

To serve, spread some whipped feta over a warm tortilla, then top with two koftas and a drizzle of harissa yoghurt. Scatter over some mint and coriander leaves, and chopped pistachios. Finish with a drizzle of pomegranate molasses and serve immediately, with lemon wedges.

SHREDDED BRISKET

1.5 kg (3 lb 5 oz) beef brisket, cut into 8 even pieces

60 ml (¼ cup) olive oil

1 large carrot, roughly diced

1 large onion, roughly diced

4–5 large garlic cloves, roughly chopped

1 tablespoon ground ancho chilli powder

2 teaspoons ground cumin

500 g (2 cups) tomato passata (pureed tomatoes)

750 ml (3 cups) beef stock

2 teaspoons apple cider vinegar

1 bay leaf

1 tablespoon dried Mexican oregano

TO SERVE

24 warm Flour tortillas (page 14), about 15 cm (6 inches) in size

Pico de gallo (page 34)

sliced avocado

Mexican crema, sour cream or creme fraiche

chopped coriander (cilantro) leaves

Green chilli sauce (page 43)

Preheat the oven to 160°C (320°F).

Season the beef well with sea salt and black pepper. Heat the olive oil in a large flameproof casserole dish (Dutch oven) over medium–high heat. Add the meat in batches, searing on all sides for 4–5 minutes, until well browned. Set the meat aside.

Turn the heat down slightly, add the carrot and onion, and cook, stirring frequently, for 5–6 minutes. Add the garlic, chilli powder and cumin, and cook for another 1–2 minutes, stirring constantly. Add the remaining ingredients, including the browned beef, then increase the heat and bring just to the boil.

Cover the dish with a tight-fitting lid, then transfer to the oven. Cook for 2½–3 hours, until the beef is fork tender. Set the meat aside, allow to cool slightly, then shred into pieces using two forks.

Place the casserole dish containing the sauce back on the stovetop over high heat. Cook for 6–7 minutes to reduce the sauce slightly, until you have about 375–500 ml (1½–2 cups) of sauce. Puree the sauce using a stick blender, then add the shredded meat and stir through to combine.

To serve, place some of the brisket on a warm tortilla. Add some pico de gallo, avocado slices, crema, coriander and a dash of green chilli sauce. Serve immediately.

CHILLI BEEF CHEEKS

1 kg (2 lb 3 oz) beef cheeks

½ teaspoon sea salt

½ teaspoon cracked black pepper

2 tablespoons olive oil

1 large onion, diced

1 bay leaf

½ cinnamon stick

750 ml (3 cups) beef stock

1 tablespoon red wine vinegar

CHILLI COOKING SAUCE

4 guajillo chillies, seeds and stems removed

3 morita chillies, seeds and stems removed

6 garlic cloves, peeled

2 teaspoons dried Mexican oregano

2 teaspoons ground cumin

2 teaspoons ground coriander

¼ teaspoon ground cloves

TO SERVE

12 warm Corn tortillas (page 15)

Pico de gallo (page 34)

Red chilli sauce (page 42)

Mexican crema, sour cream or creme fraiche

Mexican red rice (page 21)

Refried black beans (page 19)

To make the chilli cooking sauce, place a cast-iron frying pan or chargrill pan over medium–high heat and dry-roast the chillies for 15–30 seconds, turning them so they don't burn. Remove and place in a bowl, cover with boiling water and leave to rehydrate for 20 minutes. Drain, reserving 250 ml (1 cup) of the chilli soaking liquid for the sauce, then puree the chillies with the remaining chilli cooking sauce ingredients and set aside.

Season the beef cheeks with the sea salt and black pepper. Place a large flameproof casserole dish (Dutch oven) over medium–high heat, add the olive oil, then sear the beef for 5–6 minutes, until browned all over. Remove from the dish and set aside.

Saute the onion in the dish for 5–7 minutes, until golden, then add the chilli cooking sauce, bay leaf, cinnamon stick, stock and all the beef. Bring to the boil, then cover and reduce the heat to a low simmer. Cook for 2½–3 hours, until the meat is tender and easily shreds with a fork. Remove from the heat.

When cool enough to handle, shred the meat using two forks. Toss the shredded beef through the sauce, stir in the vinegar, and season with more salt and pepper to taste.

To serve, place some shredded beef on a warm tortilla, then top with pico de gallo, red chilli sauce and crema. Serve immediately, with a side of red rice and refried beans.

BEEF SHORT RIBS

4 dried pasilla chillies, seeds and stems removed

2 dried cascabel chillies, seeds and stems removed

4 chipotle chillies in adobo sauce

4 large beef short ribs on the bone, about 1.5 kg (3 lb 5 oz) in total

1 teaspoon sea salt

1 teaspoon cracked black pepper

60 ml (¼ cup) olive oil

1 large onion, sliced

4 garlic cloves, crushed

2 teaspoons ground cumin

2 teaspoons dried Mexican oregano

440 ml (15 fl oz) dark Mexican beer

750 ml (3 cups) chicken stock, approximately

CHIPOTLE CREMA

250 g (1 cup) Mexican crema, sour cream or creme fraiche

2 chipotle chillies in adobo sauce, plus 2 teaspoons of the sauce

1 tablespoon lime juice

TO SERVE

18 warm Corn tortillas (page 15)

crumbled queso fresco or mild feta

chopped onion

coriander (cilantro) leaves

lime wedges

Place a cast-iron frying pan over medium–high heat and dry-roast the dried chillies for 15–30 seconds, turning them so they don't burn. Remove and place in a bowl, cover with boiling water and leave to rehydrate for 20 minutes. Drain and place the chillies in a blender with the chipotle chillies and blitz to a puree. Set aside.

Season the beef ribs with the salt and pepper. Place a large flameproof casserole dish (Dutch oven) over medium–high heat, add the olive oil, then sear the ribs on all sides for 5–6 minutes, until browned. Remove from the dish and set aside.

Saute the onion in the dish for 6–7 minutes, until a light golden brown. Add the garlic, cumin and oregano and cook for a further minute. Return the ribs to the pan, add the pureed chillies, then pour in the beer and 500 ml (2 cups) of the chicken stock. Bring to the boil. Cover with a tight-fitting lid, reduce the heat to a low simmer and cook for 2 hours.

Check the liquid level in the dish and add the remaining 250 ml (1 cup) of stock, if needed. Simmer for a further 1–1½ hours, until the meat is cooked through, very tender and falling off the bones. Remove from the heat.

To make the chipotle crema, blitz the ingredients together in a blender and refrigerate until required; it will keep in a clean airtight container in the fridge for 4–5 days.

When cool enough to handle, shred the meat using two forks, then stir it back through the sauce. Season with more salt and pepper to taste.

To serve, place some beef mixture on a warm tortilla, then scatter over some cheese, onion and coriander. Finish with a drizzle of chipotle crema and a squeeze of lime, and serve immediately.

GOCHUJANG BEEF *and* KIMCHI

1 tablespoon toasted sesame oil

800 g (1 lb 12 oz) minced (ground) beef

3 garlic cloves, minced

2 teaspoons minced ginger

HOT WOK SAUCE

125 g (½ cup) gochujang paste

2 tablespoons honey

5 teaspoons soy sauce

4 teaspoons rice vinegar

GOCHUJANG MAYO

90 g (⅓ cup) mayonnaise

2 tablespoons gochujang paste

1 tablespoon honey

1 tablespoon lime juice

TO SERVE

14 warm small Corn tortillas (page 15)

kimchi

1 nashi pear, julienned

thinly sliced red chilli

thinly sliced spring onions (scallions)

toasted sesame seeds

Place the gochujang mayo ingredients in a bowl and whisk to combine. Taste and add more lime juice, if desired. The mayo will keep in a sealed glass container in the fridge for about 5 days.

Place a wok over high heat and add the sesame oil and beef. Cook for 3–4 minutes, using a wooden spoon to break up the meat as you toss it. Add the garlic and ginger and cook for another 1–2 minutes, until the meat has browned and is fully cooked. Toss in the hot wok sauce ingredients, stir to combine and simmer for 1–2 minutes, until slightly thickened.

To serve, spoon some of the beef mixture onto a warm tortilla and top with a little kimchi, pear and chilli. Drizzle with the gochujang mayo and finish with a sprinkling of spring onion and a pinch of toasted sesame seeds. Serve immediately.

CHIPOTLE DOUBLE-CHEESE SMASH BURGERS

600 g (1 lb 5 oz) minced (ground) beef (with 20% fat)

2 chipotle chillies in adobo sauce, finely chopped

30 g (1 oz) butter

12 slices American cheese

6 warm small Flour tortillas (page 14)

SPICY 'SPECIAL SAUCE'

125 g (½ cup) mayonnaise

3 tablespoons tomato ketchup

1 tablespoon agave syrup

1 tablespoon chipotle chillies in adobo sauce

½ teaspoon Worcestershire sauce

¼ teaspoon sweet paprika

TO SERVE

2 handfuls of shredded iceberg lettuce

pickled jalapeno chilli slices

Place the spicy 'special sauce' ingredients in a bowl and whisk well to combine; taste and add a little more chipotle chilli, if desired. The sauce will keep in a sealed glass container in the fridge for 5–7 days.

Place the beef in a bowl with the chipotle chilli and a good pinch of sea salt and black pepper. Mix until well combined. Shape into six balls, about 100 g (3½ oz) each, and set aside.

Heat a flat chargrill pan or large cast-iron frying pan over medium–high heat and add the butter. Place a beef ball on the hot surface and then, using a burger press, smash the beef until very thin and flat. Keep the pressure on and cook for 2 minutes.

Place a slice of American cheese on the burger and top with a tortilla. Reapply the press and smash down on the tortilla, then cook for a further 1 minute, or until the beef is crispy, browned and cooked through.

Flip the tortilla burger over, top with another slice of cheese, and cook for a further 1 minute or until the cheese has melted, and the other side of the tortilla is warmed a little.

To serve, top with shredded lettuce, a few pickled jalapenos and a drizzle of spicy 'special sauce'. Enjoy immediately, while it's hot and the cheese is melty.

Cook and serve the remaining smash-burger tacos in the same way.

MEATBALLS IN CHIPOTLE ADOBO SAUCE

BEEF & LAMB

100 g (3½ oz) Mexican chorizo sausage

400 g (14 oz) minced (ground) beef

90 g (½ cup) cooked medium-grain rice

1 egg

1 small onion, finely chopped

¼ cup chopped coriander (cilantro)

1 teaspoon dried Mexican oregano or regular oregano

1 teaspoon each dried epazote and ground cumin

½ teaspoon each sea salt and cracked black pepper

CHIPOTLE ADOBO SAUCE

80 ml (⅓ cup) olive oil

1 onion, diced

2 garlic cloves, finely crushed

2 × 400 g (14 oz) tins chopped tomatoes

6 chipotle chillies in adobo sauce, diced, plus 2 tablespoons of the sauce

2 teaspoons white vinegar

1 teaspoon dried Mexican oregano

TO SERVE

Mexican red rice (page 21)

Pinto beans in the pot (page 18)

8 warm Flour tortillas (page 14), about 15 cm (6 inches) in size

oregano and coriander (cilantro) leaves

Mexican crema or sour cream

lime wedges

crumbled cotija cheese

Remove and discard the casing from the chorizo sausage. Place the sausage meat and the remaining ingredients in a large bowl and mix together well. Divide the mixture into 16 equal portions and roll into balls. Place on a tray, cover and refrigerate while making the chipotle adobo sauce.

To make the chipotle adobo sauce, place a large wide saucepan over medium–low heat, add the olive oil and gently saute the onion for 8–9 minutes, until soft and translucent. Add the garlic and cook for another minute, then stir in the remaining sauce ingredients and simmer over low heat for 25 minutes. Season with salt and pepper.

Add the meatballs to the pan. Increase the heat, just bringing the sauce to the boil, then simmer over low heat for 25–30 minutes, until the meatballs are cooked through and the sauce has reduced slightly.

To serve, place some rice and beans on a warm tortilla. Top with a spoonful of sauce, then two meatballs and a bit more sauce. Scatter over some herbs, add a dollop of crema, a squeeze of lime and some crumbled cotija cheese. Serve immediately.

QUESABIRRIA

1 kg (2 lb 3 oz) chuck roast, cut into 10 cm (4 in) pieces

1.5 kg (3 lb 5 oz) beef short ribs

2 tablespoons olive oil

500 ml (2 cups) beef or chicken stock

THREE-CHILLI SAUCE

6 dried guajillo chillies

6 dried ancho chillies

5 dried arbol chillies

1 tablespoon olive oil

1 large onion, roughly chopped

8 garlic cloves, roughly chopped

1½ teaspoons ground cumin

1½ teaspoons smoked paprika

1 teaspoon cracked black pepper

1 teaspoon ground coriander

400 g (14 oz) tin crushed whole tomatoes

80 ml (⅓ cup) apple cider vinegar

2 litres (8 cups) beef or chicken stock, plus extra if needed

3 bay leaves

2 oregano sprigs

1 cinnamon stick

1 carrot, peeled but left whole

Season the beef pieces and ribs well with sea salt and black pepper. Heat the olive oil in a large flameproof casserole dish (Dutch oven) over medium heat. When hot, sear the beef and ribs, in batches, for 8–10 minutes, until well browned on all sides. Remove the meat from the dish and set aside, but don't clean out the dish.

Preheat the oven to 150°C (300°F).

To make the three-chilli sauce, warm a cast-iron frying pan over low heat and dry-fry the chillies, in batches, for 1 minute each side, taking care not to burn the skin. Remove and set aside. When cool enough to handle, discard the stems and seeds.

Place the casserole dish back over medium heat, adding the oil to the beef drippings in the dish. Stir the onion through and saute for about 4 minutes. Add the garlic and cook for a further 1–2 minutes, until the onion is soft. Stir in the toasted chillies, ground spices, tomatoes, vinegar and 1 litre (4 cups) of the stock. Cook for about 20 minutes, until the chillies are soft.

Remove from the heat and puree the sauce using a stick blender until smooth. Add the seared beef and ribs, and any residual meat juices, along with the bay leaves, oregano, cinnamon stick and whole carrot. Pour in the remaining stock and put the lid on.

Braise in the oven for 3½–4 hours, until the meat is falling off the ribs. Check the dish after 3 hours, and add a little more stock or water if needed.

Remove the dish from the oven. Remove the meat, discard the bones and shred the meat using two forks. Discard any sinew that hasn't melted down.

Pour the sauce through a sieve and discard the herbs, cinnamon stick and carrot.

30 Corn tortillas (page 15)

600 g (1 lb 5 oz) oaxaca cheese or mozzarella, shredded, or 30 slices Monterey jack

½ cup chopped coriander (cilantro) leaves

Mix about 250 ml (1 cup) of the sauce through the shredded meat, so it is rich and juicy. Season with sea salt if needed.

Now pour the remaining sauce back into the dish, and stir in the 500 ml (2 cups) of stock; you want this sauce to be a bit broth-like, and thin enough to dip your tacos into. There will be quite a bit of fat on the surface, which is exactly the desired result.

Place the dish back over low heat to keep warm while you assemble your tacos.

Heat a flat chargrill pan or large frying pan over medium heat. Dip each tortilla, one by one, into the fat sitting on the top of the sauce, covering the tortilla in the orange-red fat. Place the tortilla in the hot pan and top with about 20 g (¾ oz) of the cheese and 50 g (1¾ oz) of the shredded meat. Cook for 30 seconds, then fold the tortilla in half and fry for a further 1–2 minutes. Flip and fry the other side for 1–2 minutes, until the cheese is melted and gooey, and the meat is crispy and golden.

Continue with the remaining tortillas, cheese and meat.

Serve immediately, with a side dish of the warm brothy sauce, sprinkled with the coriander.

INDEX

Published in 2024 by Smith Street Books
Naarm (Melbourne) | Australia
smithstreetbooks.com

ISBN: 978-1-9230-4929-1

Smith Street Books respectfully acknowledges the Wurundjeri People of the Kulin Nation, who are the Traditional Owners of the land on which we work, and we pay our respects to their Elders past and present.

Publishing director: Paul McNally
Managing editor: Lucy Heaver
Editor: Katri Hilden
Design and illustrations: George Saad
Typesetter: Megan Ellis
Photography: Mark Roper
Food styling: Deborah Kaloper
Food preparation: Caroline Griffiths and Meryl Batlle
Proofreader: Pamela Dunne
Indexer: Helena Holmgren

Printed & bound in China by C&C Offset Printing Co., Ltd.

Some of the recipes in this book were first published in *Taco-topia* in 2018, by Smith Street Books.

Book 332
10 9 8 7 6 5 4